ENTREPRENEURSHIP TEXT AND CASES

ENTREPRENEURSHIP TEXT AND CASES

Bidyadhar Behera

MJP Publishers

Chennai   New Delhi   Tirunelveli

ISBN 978-81-8094-215-0 **MJP Publishers**

All rights reserved
Printed and bound in India

New No. 5 Muthu Kalathy Street,
Triplicane,
Chennai 600 005

MJP 176   © Publishers, 2014

Publisher : J.C. Pillai

For Papa and Maa who give me strength.
For loving Aru, Mom and Tapan who
accept me as I am.

Preface

Entrepreneurship is a testament of the progressive and inclusive growth perception of an economy. It stimulates competition while providing positive vibes for economic development. Entrepreneurship across the nation-states has assumed special significance regardless of their stages of development. While, high entrepreneurial index reflects the level of economic progress, the objective of industrial development, regional growth and employment generation depend very much upon entrepreneurial development. As the vehicle of industrial development, entrepreneurship solves problems, such as, unemployment, concentration of economic power, increasing wastage of youth power in destructive activities, etc. Today, both men and women are increasingly embracing entrepreneurship as their life style. In fact, it proves to be the de facto barometer of overall economic, social and industrial growth. In the process, entrepreneurship has been riding the crest of total wave length of popularity. With land being the main source of livelihood in rural areas, be it agriculture, animal husbandry, forestry and allied activities, India has emerged as one of the fastest growing economies. Witnessing a steady GDP growth, its pace of growth is not homogenous all through. Rural India is unable to match the speed of development and growth of urban India. It may be hypothesised here that India is not a poor country, but a poorly-managed country. While it is poised to become one of the youngest nations in the world in a couple of years, it is the youth who has to largely shoulder the responsibility of saving the environment. This can be possible only if they start making smaller changes in their occupational engagements and lifestyles that could lead to a ripple effect.

Entrepreneurs are the seeds of industrial development, while the fruits of industrial development include greater employment opportunities, increased per capita income, higher standard of living, revenue to the government in terms of income tax, sales tax, export duties, import duties and balanced regional development. In practice, entrepreneurs have historically altered the direction of national economies, industries, or markets. They have invented new products and developed organizations and the means of production to bring them to market. They have, indeed, introduced quantum leaps in technology and more productive uses. For instance, techno entrepreneurs like Steve Jobs have forced the reallocation of resources away from existing users to new and more productive users.

Further, entrepreneurship is typically a choice for those who belong to business families, for those who wish to be independent, to achieve something personally and also for staving off unemployment. India has 45 million entrepreneurs-most building small businesses, some building big businesses-but all contributing to an economy that boasts a middle class as big as the entire population of the United States. The economic trends, at present, kindle the hope that if India develops a right roadmap for facing the global competition, it can once again regain its past glory as a prosperous nation. Against this backdrop, the present book provides an opportunity for those with experience and imagination to test their ideas by sharing with a larger peer group that demonstrates commitment to the cause of entrepreneurship and the MSMEs. The target audiences are entrepreneurs, small business executives, family business leaders, policy makers, intervention agencies, researchers and academics among others. The readers who are interested in working in small businesses, entrepreneurial ventures, or not-for-profit organisations will find the description of entrepreneurship concepts applicable to their needs because the book includes examples and case studies from a broad spectrum of organizations. The book will give, within a short compass, a good idea of the subject to the beginners. In fact, it reflects an humble attempt through a writing style that readers will find interesting and straight forward to meet these ends.

Given the diverse nature of audiences and their requirements, a lucid presentation of the cases in the book speak for themselves. For incorporating suitable cases, the author has drawn cues from the decision of IIM-Khozikode introducing subjects like liberal art in its MBA programme where clientele largely constitute the engineering students. There, the reason is art and science of management is the art and science of decision-making. Though the engineering graduates are strong in analytical skill, they, as the crucial decision makers should be equally familiar with the works like O'thello, Sherlok Holmes, Ramayan and Mahabharat and those produced by Rabindra Nath Tagore, Aristotle, Shakeshpere. For, as sometimes, rues by the Dean, IIM-K, their decisions must influence the heart, not the mind only. Hence, the lively and contemporary cases, small and big alike have been cited in each chapter based on international and domestic experiences.

Last but not the least, the author deems it as a pleasure to request the fraternity members as well as the students to give their invaluable feedback for further improvement of the book.

Bidyadhar Behera

Acknoweldgement

At the outset, I would like to apreciate and remember the inspiration drawn from a good number of my well wishers both within and outside India. I am indebted to my beloved parents for their kind words of encouragement in completing this noble assignment. I also thank my wife, Aruna and daughter, Suranjika for their cooperation in accomplishing this task. Besides, I am thankful to the researchers, authors of books, publishers and editors, whose publications have materially helped me in drafting this work.

Contents

1

ENTREPRENEURSHIP

INTRODUCTION

Entrepreneurship is a testament of the progressive and inclusive growth perception of an economy. It serves as the foundation of an economy while stimulating competition. It also provides positive vibes for economic development. Entrepreneurship across the nation-states has assumed special significance regardless of the stages of development. Besides, high entrepreneurial index reflects the level of economic progress. Needless to say, the objective of industrial development, regional growth and employment generation depend very much upon entrepreneurial development. In fact, the question of enhancing entrepreneurship in the new and competitive global era has been a concern for the academicians, researchers and policy makers. The stress is on how to create sustainable and resilient businesses and develop entrepreneurship in the growing economies. In the current economy, giant corporations are right-sizing, restructuring and reducing layers of management while jobs are being eliminated. Some departments of these businesses are being hived off, whereas many home-based businesses are springing up. At the same time, some of these have contracts with large businesses to provide services they now outsource. While on one hand jobs are being lost, on the other hand more jobs are being created than were never before through entrepreneurship. Moreover, falling trade barriers, improved communications, the internet and globalization have facilitated creation of new ventures worldwide. It has ushered in an era of unprecedented collaboration and inter-global communication and influence, unlike anything we have ever seen.

Entrepreneurship is typically a choice for those who belong to business families, for those who wish to be independent, to achieve something personally and also for staving off unemployment. In essence, entrepreneurship is motivated by the drive to meet personal, emotional, or financial needs. It combines many qualities such as innovation, risk taking, organising factors of production, etc. Undoubtedly, it depends on personal qualities like accepting the challenge and bearing the risk. While men as well as women are increasingly embracing entrepreneurship as their lifestyle, it is the de facto barometer of overall economic, social and industrial growth. Today's knowledge-worker expects to work in an environment, that is peer-to-peer, not hierarchial. They want to express their intelligence, not be told what to do. India being one among the youngest nations in the world, in a couple of years, its youth needs to largely shoulder the responsibility of saving the socio-economic environment. This can be possible only if they start making smaller changes in their occupational engagements and lifestyles that could lead to a ripple effect.

Entrepreneurship plays a critical role in the growth of an economy. Besides being the vehicle of industrial development, it solves problems, such as, unemployment, imbalanced regional development, concentration of economic power, increasing wastage of youth power in destructive activities, etc. In the process, entrepreneurship has been riding the crest of total wavelength of popularity. It is, in fact, the ability to identify an investment opportunity and to organize an enterprise in order to contribute for the real economic growth. In a nutshell, it is the function of handling economic activity, undertaking risk, creating something new while organizing and coordinating resources.

DEFINITIONS

The concept of entrepreneurship has long been debated and used in various ways and various senses. Both, entrepreneurship and entrepreneur have been used synonymously. According to A.H. Cole, entrepreneurship is the purposeful activity of an individual or a group of associated individuals, undertaken to initiate, maintain or earn profit by production or distribution of economic goods and services. In the words of A. Thomas, entrepreneurship is the ability to create or build something from practically nothing. Fundamentally, a human creative activity, it is finding personal energy by initiating, building and achieving an enterprise or organization rather than just watching, analysing or describing one. It requires the ability to take risk and to reduce the chance of failure. It is the knack of sensing an opportunity where others see chaos, contradiction and confusion. It is the know-how to find, marshal and control resources and to make sure the venture does not run out of money when it is needed the most.

IMPORTANCE OF ENTREPRENEURSHIP

Entrepreneurial development today has assumed special siginificance, since it is a key to economic development The objective of industrial development, regional growth and employment generation depend upon entrepreneurial development. As Peter F Drucher has aptly put, "Entrepreneurship is neither a science nor an art. It is a practice having a knowledge base. Knowledge in entrepreneurship is the means to an end. Indeed, what constitutes knowledge in practice is largely defined by the ends, that is by practice." Entrepreneurship is meant for creating something new, organizing and coordinating and undertaking risk and handling economic uncertainty.

According to B. Higgins, "Entrepreneurship meant the function of seeking investment and production opportunity, organizing an enterprise to undertake a new production process, raising capital, hiring labour, arranging the supply of raw materials, finding site, introducing new techniques and commodities, discovering new sources of raw materials, selecting top managers of day to day operations of the enterprise." Many innovations have transformed the society and changed our pattern of living and many services have been introduced to alter or create new service industries. Entrepreneurship while playing an important role in the development of society through facilitating large scale production and distribution of goods and services, has also widened the scope of their marketing.

DISTINCTION BETWEEN ENTREPRENEUR AND ENTREPRENEURSHIP

Most often the terms entrepreneur and entrepreneurship are used interchangeably. Yet they are conceptually different.

However, the following table helps us to understand the distinction between an entrepreneur and entrepreneurship.

Entrepreneurship	Entreprepreneur
Entrepreneurship is a plan of action.	Entrepreneur is a person.
Entrepreneurship is an administration.	Entrepreneur is an administrator.
It is a risk-bearing activity.	Entrepreneur is a risk-bearer.
It is a process of innovation.	Entrepreneur is an innovator.
It is the process of using of factors of production.	Entrepreneur combines the factors of production.
Entrepreneurship is taking an initiative.	Entrepreneur is an initiator.
Entrepreneurship is nothing but leadership	

Thus, entrepreneurship refers to a process whereby ideas and innovations are converted into action, whereas, entrepreneur is a person. Entrepreneurial functions are collectively termed as entrepreneurship. Entrepreneurship without entrepreneur is unthinkable while entrepreneurship is the action part of an entrepreneur.

CHARACTERISTICS OF ENTREPRENEURSHIP

Considerable effort has gone into understanding the psychological and sociological wellsprings of entrepreneurship; and some common characteristics like the need for achievement, locus of control, orientation towards intuitive thinking, and risk-taking propensity of entrepreneurs have been suggested. This raises the question as: Can these traits be generalized

....

across countries and culture? In the current scenario, we have a broad spectrum of different countries with respect to the economic structure as well as the stage of economic status therein. However, entrepreneurship is more complex and a multidimensional subject with the following important features:

Innovation According to certain business literature, an idea, a change or an improvement is only an innovation when it is put to use and effectively causes a social or commercial reorganization. Entrepreneur does things in a new and better way. This makes an entrepreneur to innovate new things, new methods and look for new markets. Entrepreneurship is a creative activity. Innovation is problem-solving, entrepreneur is a problem-solver and entrepreneurship is the process of putting innovation into use.

Decision-making Doing things in a new and better manner leads to innovation. In addition to innovation, entrepreneur has to take decisions under uncertainty. Entrepreneurship is a function of high achievement. Achievement motive can be increased considerably by deliberate efforts.

Building the organization According to Frederick Harbison, entrepreneurship implies the skill to build an organization. Building an organization requires lot of skills and one can build an organization effectively by delegating responsibility to others. Hence, entrepreneurs should be good leaders.

Managerial skills Managerial skills and leadership are the most important characteristics of entrepreneurship. B.F. Hoselitz maintains that a person who is to become an industrial entrepreneur must have more than mere drive to earn profits in order to amass wealth. He must have the ability to lead and manage.

Resource mobilization An entrepreneur's job is to fill the gaps. Through mobilization of resources, an entrepreneur has to marshal all the inputs to realize final product. According to H. Libenstein, the supply of entrepreneurship is governed by input completing capacity.

ENTREPRENEURSHIP AS A PROCESS

Entrepreneurship is a process consisting of the following stages:

Stage 1   Change in the real world. Any change in the socio-economic environment may reflect in the lifestyles. Change in the lifestyle necessitates new products. However, new products are developed through new ideas.

Stage 2   New environment, new lifestyles ask for new ideas. New product ideas can be derived from many sources like customers and competitors. Good ideas come from inspiration, perspiration and techniques. Ideas generated are to be screened to drop poor ideas as early as possible.

Stage 3   After screening the ideas, the short listed ideas are to be developed into products. To develop ideas into products, an entrepreneur has to start his venture. Starting a new venture is the third stage.

Stage 4   Mobilization of internal resources is the next stage in the process of entrepreneurship. Use of internal resources may also be known as entrepreneurship.

Stage 5   An entrepreneur has to co-ordinate and organize various activities to achieve the organizational goals. The co-ordination of various activities is the last stage.

There may be various ways through which one may become an entrepreneur, such as acquiring a running enterprise, starting a new business, acquiring a franchise, i.e., running a business based on the right to manufacture something granted by a manufacturer or other organization.

BARRIERS TO ENTREPREUNEURSHIP

There may be several factors responsible for the failure of new product or new venture. Many entrepreneurs fail due to several barriers which include:

    i.   The idea is good but the market size is over-estimated or

    ii.   Idea is pushed through without any research being carried on or

    iii.   Actual product is not designed as well as it should be or

    iv.   It is incorrectly positioned in the market and, or

    v.   It is over-priced, etc.

Karl H. Vasper, in Entrepreneurship and National Policy has identified the following barriers.

- Lack of viable project/concept
- Lack of market knowledge
- Lack of technical skills
- Lack of initial capital
- Lack of business knowledge
- Complacency—lack of motivation
- Social stigma
- Time pressures and distractions
- Legal constraints and regulations
- Monopoly and protectionism
- Inhibitions due to patents

Bilayati Kirana: A Case of Family Enterprise

This case study brings home to the readers some contextual revelations in view of the recent debate in the floor of Indian Parliament due to the favourable stand taken by the Government as regards Foreign Direct Investment (FDI) in the retail sector. The study projects a personal experience of a leading Indian columnist, Mr. Jug Suraiya about a mom-and-pop shop in London. In his words, "I wonder what the regular customers of Hughes Stores would have made of the current ruckus going on in India about FDI in retail and how it will wipe out the kirana stores, the equivalent of the West's mom-and-pop shops". Hughes Stores was a Bilayati kirana shop in the London suburb of Harrow. Its ownership was held by an Indian, Mrs. Vasu and her husband, Babu from a Mr. Hughes. Running a kirana store is, undoubtedly, a hard work, as noticed by Jug, the brother of Vasu. During his trip to London in 1976, Jug visited Hughes store. It was a delivery day. A large van was parked in front of the shop. The driver was unloading goods from the wholesale warehouse and piling them on the pavement. From here, the boxes and crates had to be carried into the store, unpacked, and their contents put on the shelves.

While Babu and Vasu did the unpacking and shelving, they'd hired a couple of college kids to do the heavy work of lugging the boxes into the shop. To help out, Jug joined with young students. Hughes Stores was a family enterprise, in which all the family pitched into help. Vasu was later found chatting with the customers as they came upto pay: How are you today, luv? Got over that nasty cold you had last week, I am glad to see. And, how is your daughter doing at university? This was Hughes Stores—and the thousands of such across the country—had to offer which the big supermarket chains did not: conversation and human contact, no matter how brief. Each customer was a known face, a remembered name. And in an increasingly impersonal society, where anonymity is the norm, this made all the difference. The regulars at Hughes did the major part of their shopping at the nearest Safeway, where the prices were more competitive. But it seemed that there was always last minute purchases to be made. Or days on which you did not want to take car out and drive all the way to the supermarket. Or times when you did not really need anything as such except a few moments of friendly chat. And for all these occasions and all these reasons, Hughes Stores retained its loyal customers who kept it in business. Babu and Vasu sold off Hughes Stores a long time ago. But, in view of Jug, it still keeps running, not in competition with supermarket but as complementary to them. It made economic sense to go to the supermarket to get the bulk of the week's groceries. But where'd you go to pick up a carton of milk, a loaf of bread, a bar of chockolate, knowing that these were just excuses, the real thing you came for being that you wanted to hear how you looked much better having got over that nasty cold, and was not it lovely that your daughter was coming home for holidays? How do you put an MRP on that?

ENTREPRENEURIAL OPPORTUNITIES IN INDIA

Entrepreneurship is related to personality, while, entrepreneurs necessarily belong to a special class. Every economy requires true entrepreneurs, who do not need incentives, infrastructure, government support but build their own enterprise, acquire the resources and develop. All this requires the adoption of value driven corporate philosophy. Quite a few, at least are good at self-goals. Hundreds of thousands of young college graduates have found jobs in the BPO sector. These are jobs that simply did not exist before. If the BPO sector had not happened, many of these Indians would have been jobless. That it happened could prove that Indian entrepreneurship can quickly take advantage of new opportunities. BPO/IT is one field where China concedes India's superiority. Further, since liberalization in India is going to complete two decades in 2011, it has completely transformed the nation's economy, pushing it into the league of the fastest growing economies in the world. It provides consumers a wide choice while unfolding new horizons of international trade for the market and opening vistas of foreign markets for the diversified product line. Though India's foreign trade constitutes only about one per cent of the total world trade, the volume and diversity is significant. Moreover, with introduction of the 1991 Economic Policy, successive governments have since carried forward the reform process, strengthening the private sector, which now contributes almost 80 per cent to the country's economy.

According to the Planning Commission Advisor, "Unshackling entrepreneurship in India is the greatest achievement of the liberalization process." The once competition-shy Indian corporate sector has come into its own and taken on global players. That is not all. Indian firms have gone ahead. They have acquired global companies, such as, Tata Steel's acquisition of Corus and, earlier, Bharati Airtel's buyout of the African operations of Kuwait's Zain. It is equally noteworthy that liberalization of trade policy and abolishing of import licensing have resulted in increased trade. Walk into any shopping mall in any small or large city, you will see top global brands jostling for space. As a consequence, international trade and business as well give tremendous scope in terms of employment and entrepreneurial opportunities in India.

A case of Spice Business

Encouraged by his father, then a small hotelier, Sarat Kumar Sahoo, the founder of Ruchi masala opted for entrepreneurial training in the period from 1970–72 after completing his intermediate studies. He joined a company preparing masala in Kolkata. In 1975, Sahoo established Ruchi brand with a view to provide unique Indian spices a definite brand. After a maiden beginning in Odisha and later making its presence felt across the country, Ruchi has crossed the border and reached markets like that of Dubai, Kuwait, Tanzania, Singapore and USA. The road to Sahoo's success has never been a path of roses. Lot of obstacles were encountered by him. His father's hotel was demolished only a day after it was redone with an investment of fifteen crore rupees due to the Super Cyclone across Indian eastern coast in the year 1999.

Fields like entrepreneurship in tourism provides broad as well as ever expanding scope for taking the socio-economic status of a region to a new height. The case studies that follow prove to be an apt case of entrepreneurship in Odisha.

2

THE ENTREPRENEUR

INTRODUCTION

Fortunately, today's knowledge-based economy serves as a fertile ground for an entrepreneur. Entrepreneur is a potential and enterprising individual, endowed with special ability to innovate or imitate and for decision making, interested in advancing technology and willingness to assume risk involved in it.

> **"My son is now an 'entrepreneur'. That's what you're called when you don't have a job."**
>
> -Ted Turner, Broadcasting entrepreneur.

What is entrepreneurship? Who are entrepreneurs? How are they different from non-entrepreneurs? Is entrepreneurship just another career option? Drawing from research, people choose entrepreneurial careers because of the perceived greater economic and psychological rewards than regular employment. Entrepreneurs are starting their enterprises to make more profits by way of producing or of marketing goods and services to cater to the needs of customers. Anyone who runs a small, medium or large business is an entrepreneur. It could be an independent operator or one who works as part of a team or in a partnership. An entrepreneur is thus someone who organizes, manages and assumes risks of a business or enterprise. However, the definition of an entrepreneur has evolved in last three centuries, from someone who bears risk by buying at a low price and selling at a higher price to the creation of new enterprises of which the entrepreneur is the founder.

India needs entrepreneurs. They need them for two reasons: to cash in on new opportunities and create wealth and new jobs. Here, it may be quite relevant to note the estimate of a report by Mckinsey & Company-Nasscom. The Report suggests that 110–130 million citizens in India will be searching for jobs by 2015, including 80–100 million looking for their first jobs which is more than seven times that of Australia's population. This, however, does not include disguised unemployment of over 50 per cent among 230 million employed in rural India. Since traditional large employers— including the Government and the old economy players— may find it difficult to sustain this level of employment in the future, it is the role of entrepreneurs to create these new jobs and opportunities.

Entrepreneurs do things that are not generally done in the ordinary course of business. Though this is a conclusion derived from "The Theory of Economic Development", authored by Joseph Schumpeter which is incomplete, it contains the essence of entrepreneurial activity. This also brings home a fact that why we are sometimes baffled by entrepreneurs who seem to be out of step with the rest of the people. Some are inspired tinkerers, an attribute ascribed to Thomas Edison, and others are gifted dreamers, a phrase once used to describe Steven Jobs. Most entrepreneurs are thought to be, simply, "unusual"; they lead their own parade, listen to their own music and set their own cadence. Consequently they do unexpected things. While entrepreneur is the engine of economic endeavour that drives industrial democracy. However, the word entrepreneur is derived from the French word "entreprendre" which refers to undertake, i.e., individuals who undertake the risk of new enterprise. Today, we take it for that the word entrepreneur suggests spirit, zeal, ideas, diversity, etc. But we tend to apply the work loosely to describe it as any one who runs the business, for example, the person who presides over a multinational company or owns a cyber cafe, shoe-stand, or who owns a tea stall. In the past, the word entrepreneur enjoyed purer and more precise meaning. It described only those who created their own business. Many entrepreneurs become celebrities through their successes, others become ridiculed for their failed dreams. But, undoubtedly, all of them contribute to the spirit and vigour of entrepreneurship in a nation.

The American Heritage Dictionary defines an entrepreneur as a person who organizes, operates and assumes the risk for a business venture. Oxford English Dictionary (in 1897) defined entrepreneur simply as the director or manager of a public musical institution, one who gets up entertainments especially music performance. In the early 16th century the French men who organized and led military expeditions were referred to as entrepreneurs. Later in the 18th century, the term was used to other types of adventures, and civil engineering works like construction of roads, buildings, bridges, etc.

The word entrepreneur has been interestingly explained by the following economists and entrepreneurs.

DEFINITION

i. Adam Smith

Adam Smith, the father of political economy, opined that entrepreneur has a role of an industrialist. In his popular book, the Wealth of Nations, he explained the entrepreneur as an individual who forms an organization for commercial purpose. He is a proprietary capitalist, a supplier of capital and at the same time, a manager who coordinates labour and consumer. He also treated the entrepreneur as an employer, master, merchant and more explicitly considered him as a capitalist. Entrepreneur is considered as one who has unusual foresight to recognize potential demand of goods and services. He transforms potential demand into supply. He possesses certain arts and skills of creating new economic enterprises. He is a person with exceptional insight into the society's needs and possesses the abilities to fulfil them satisfactorily. Thus, he is perceived as "Economic Risk Taker" of Cantillon and "Industrial Manager" of Adam Smith.

ii. Richard Cantillon

Cantillon, an Irishman living in France in the early 18th century used the word entrepreneur for the first time in his writings. He is considered as pioneer for the introduction of the word entrepreneur. According to him, entrepreneur is a person who pays certain price for a product to resell it at an uncertain price thereby making decision about attaining and using resources while assuming the risk of enterprise. Hence he is conceived as bearer of non-insurable risk. Cantillon opines that entrepreneur's function is to combine factors of production into a producing organism. Entrepreneurs make very conscious decisions regarding resource allocation for high commercial gain. Therefore, Cantillon's definition of entrepreneur clearly envisages that entrepreneur carries out production and exchange of goods at some risk when the demand for the product declines. He also emphasised that the entrepreneur would be unaware of the price which he gets for his products.

iii. J.B. Say

The ideas of Cantillon have been expanded by another Frenchman J.B. Say. According to him, an entrepreneur is the economic agent who unites all the means of production, the labour force, the capital or land of the others and who finds the value of product that results from their employment, the reconstitution of the entire capital that he utilizes and the value of the wages, the interest and the rent which he pays as well as profit belonging to himself. Say emphasized on bringing together of all factors of production and the provision of continuing management as well as risk-bearing. He opined that entrepreneur may or may not possess the capital but he must have the quality of judgment, perseverance and knowledge of global business. Thus, the entrepreneur is considered as an organizer of the business firm, central to its distributive and productive functions.

iv. Bernard F. De Bolidar

Bernard F. De Bolidar defined entrepreneur as a person who performs the task of briging labour and material at certain price and selling the resultant product at a contracted price. This definition of F. De Bolidar resembles the definition of J.B. Say wherein he laid emphasis on bringing together of the factors of production. The contract price depends on the demand, supply position of the market and bargaining capacities of the parties concerned.

v. F.H. Knight

According to Knight, entrepreneurs are a specialized group of persons who undertake the risk and deal with uncertainty. Entrepreneur is the economic functionary who undertakes responsibility which cannot be insured. Knight tried to differentiate risk and uncertainty. A risk can be insured through the principle of insurance whereas uncertainty is the risk which cannot be calculated. According to Knight, the entrepreneur must possess the qualities of ability, willingness and power to guarantee specific sums to others in return for the assignments made to him.

vi. Carl Menger

As aptly put by an Australian, Carl Menger, economic changes do not arise from the circumstances but from the individual's awareness and understanding of the circumstances. He was of the view that entrepreneur transforms the available resources into useful goods and services. Menger's classic theory of production indicates that resources having no direct use in terms of fulfilling human needs were transformed into highly valuable products and services that directly fulfills the human needs. Thus, the transformation of resources into useful goods and services creates the circumstances leading to industrial growth and entrepreneur is rewarded with profits.

Vii. E.E. Hagen

According to E.E. Hagen, entrepreneur is an economic man, who tries to maximize his profits by undertaking innovations.

Innovations involve problem-solving and he gets satisfaction from using capabilities in solving such problems.

viii. Francis A. Walker

F.A. Walker puts entrepreneur is one who is endowed with more than average capacities in the task of organization and co-ordinating the factors of production, i.e., land, labour, capital and enterprise. Entrepreneur is a pioneer, a leader, and a captain of the firm. Hence, the profit earned by the entrepreneur depends on his efficiency and superior talent.

ix. David C. McClelland

According to David C. McClelland, entrepreneur is one who takes decision under uncertainty and does things in a new and innovative way to get the desired profit. He opined that entrepreneur must prefer personal responsibility for decisions and he should be a moderate risk- taker. He must also possess interest in concrete knowledge of the results of the decisions. McClelland opines that the need for achievement drives people to become entrepreneurs.

x. Joseph Schumpeter

Joseph Schumpeter described an entrepreneur as one who seeks to reform or revolutionize the pattern of production by exploiting an innovation or more generally, an untried technological possibility for producing a new commodity or producing an old one in a new way, by opening up a new source of supply of material or a new outlet of products. Thus, Schumpeter's theory views the potential profitable opportunities and exploits them. He is of the view that an entrepreneur does not only desire to raise his consumption standard by earning handsome profits but aspires to find a private dynasty. Therefore, according to

Schumpeter, an entrepreneur is one who innovates, raises money, collects inputs, organizes talent, provides leadership and sets the organization. Schumpeter, for the first time in 1934, assigned an important role of innovation to the entrepreneur. He did not equate entrepreneur with an inventor. An inventor creates a new product while Schumpeter's entrepreneur exists if the factors of production are combined for the first time. A distrinction between an inventory and innovator has also been made by Schumpeter. Inventor discovers new methods and raw materials and an innovator utilizes discoveries in order to make new combinations. According to Schumpeter, innovation leads to the introduction of a new product in the market, the instituting of new production technology which has not yet been tested, bringing in new quality of product, expansion of the market by entering into new markets into which the specific product has not entered so far, discovery of new source of supply of raw materials and helps in carrying out a new form of organization of a business venture. However, the theory propounded by Schumpeter's theory is based on the following assumptions;

i.   Existence of sufficient availability of capital,

ii.   Existence of developed banking system to avoid scarcity of capital.

iii.   Existence of a high-level developed technology,

iv.   Existence of private initiative, and broad-based entrepreneurial process.

In view of the above assumptions, it can be inferred that Schumpeter's theory is more applicable in a developed economy and it may not be suitable for the underdeveloped economy. It is because in underdeveloped economies, the path of innovativeness is blocked by scarcity of capital and other facilities.

xi. Peter F. Drucker

As per Peter F. Drucker, entrepreneurial role is one of getting and using resources. According to him, an entrepreneur is one who always searches. According to Drucker, an entrepreneur is one who always searches for change, responds to it and exploits it as an opportunity. Innovation is considered as an instrument of entrepreneurship. An entrepreneur innovates and creates resources because there is no such thing as resource until somebody finds a use for something and endows economic value to it. Innovation is being presented as a discipline, capable of being learnt and capable of being practiced. Entrepreneurs need to search purposefully for the sources of innovation, the changes and their symptoms that indicate opportunities for successful innovation. Thus, Peter F. Drucker has clearly envisaged the role of entrepreneur in the following words:

- An entrepreneur must be an innovator as well as a leader also.

- He must be capable of analysing the opportunities and exploit them successfully.

- He should innovate for the present period but not for the future.

- Innovation must be very simple to understand, otherwise it may not give the desired results.

- He must possess the knowledge, ingenuity, diligence, persistence and commitment to innovation.

- He need not be the owner of the business.

- He must mobilize resources and allocate them to make a commercial gain from the opportunities identified.

Thus, Drucker considers an entrepreneur as one who always searches for change, responds to it and exploits it as an opportunity.

xii. Encyclopedia Britannica

It has defined entrepreneur as an individual who bears the risk of operating a business in the face of uncertainty about future conditions.

xiii. International Labour Organisation

It has described entrepreneurs as those people who have the ability to see and evaluate business opportunities, together the necessary resources to take advantage of them and to initiate appropriate action to ensure success.

xiv. Webster's New World Dictionary

Webster's New World Dictionary of American language defined entrepreneur as one who organizes the business undertaking, assuming the risk for the sake of profit.

On the basis of the above definitions, it can be concluded that an entrepreneur is one who conceives an enterprise for the purpose, displays required initiative, grit and determination to bring the project into action. In the process of bringing the new project into the market, the entrepreneur undertakes number of responsibilities such as perceiving opportunities for profitable investments, explores the prospects of starting a enterprise, obtains the license, arranges the required initial capital, provides personal guarantees to the financial institutions, supplies the required technical know-how, etc. Thus, entrepreneur is an economic agent who unites all means of production to maximize his profits by innovations.

NATURE AND IMPORTANCE OF ENTREPRENEUR

Entrepreneurs play a vital role in economic development. Economic development is essentially a process to increase the real per capita income of the country over a period of time. Entrepreneurs serve as catalysts in the process of industrialization and economic growth. He puts to use capital, labour and technology and acts as an economic agent. According to Joseph Schumpeter, the rate of economic progress of a nation depends upon its rate of innovation which is turn depends on rate of increase in the entrepreneurial talent in the population. According to Meir and Baldwin, development does not occur spontaneously as a natural consequence when economic conditions in some sense are right. A catalyst is needed which results in entrepreneurial activity to a considerable extent, the diversity of activities that characterizes rich countries can be attributed to the supply of entrepreneurs. Thus, entrepreneurs are key to the creation of enterprises. They play a vital role for the economic development of a country in the following ways:

1. Formation of Capital

Entrepreneur's efforts to mobilize the capital results in motivating the investors to divert their idle savings in the industrial securities. Investment of public money in industrial sector helps the country to use such resources for productive purposes. The growth rate of capital formation will be increased which is highly essential for rapid economic development of a country. Robert Rostand has rightly said that entrepreneur is the creator of wealth. It is in this sense that entrepreneurs generate the capital at a rapid rate and capital formation increases which is vital for the industrial development.

2. Balanced Regional Development

Entrepreneurs in the public and private sectors help to remove regional disparities by setting up industries in the backward areas. It is because the government extend various concessions and subsidies to the entrepreneurs who take initiatives to set up industries in the undeveloped regions. Thus, the central and stage governments offer of concessions and subsidies to the entrepreneurs results in balanced regional development.

3. Generates Employment

Entrepreneurs help in generating employment directly and indirectly. Entrepreneur becomes self-employed and becomes self-sufficient and lead a honorable life. They do not depend on the government jobs or private jobs and directly employ themselves by starting their own enterprise. Indirectly, they also provide jobs to many unemployed by setting up large- and small-scale industries. Thus, entrepreneurs play an important role to reduce the unemployment problem in the country and pave the way for economic development.

4. Improvement of Per Captial Income

Entrepreneurs have the skills of locating and identifying the opportunities to establish their own enterprises. They possess the capacities to convert the latent and idle resources like land, labour and capital into goods and services. This will result in increase in the national income and wealth of a nation. The increase in national income is the indication of increase in net national product and per capita income of the country. The increasing tendency reflects the economic growth and industrialization that is taking place in the nation.

5. Improvement of Standard of Living

The initiative taken by entrepreneurs to set up industries helps in removing scarcity of essential commodities. New products, varied products and qualitative products would be manufactured to suit the requirements of different segments of market. Large-scale production helps to offer goods at a lower costs and purchasing power of the consumers also increases. Further, the small-scale industries set up by entrepreneurs help to avoid scarcity of goods and improve the standard of living of the consumers. Thus, the efforts of entrepreneurs to set up large-scale and small-scale industries, offer goods at lower price to the consumers and increase variety in their consumption.

6. National Self-Reliance

Entrepreneurs are very much required for national self-reliance. It is because they help to manufacture indigenous substitutes to imported products which reduce the dependence on foreign countries. There is also a possibility of exporting goods and services which leads to earning of foreign exchange for the country. Hence, the import substitution and export promotion ensure economic independence and the country will become self-reliant.

7. Planning Production

Entrepreneurs are considered as economic agents since they unite all means of production. All the factors of production, i.e., land, labour, capital and enterprise are brought together to get the desired production. This will help to make use all the factors of production with a proper judgment, perseverance and with a knowledge of the world of business. Thus, a true entrepreneur is endowed with more than average capacities in the task or organizing and co-ordinating the various factors of production to get higher profits for his enterprise.

8. Backward and Forward Linkages

Always the entrepreneur initiates change and tries to maximize his profits by innovations. Setting up of an enterprise in accordance with the changing technology, has several backward and forward linkages. For example, the establishment of textile unit generates several ancillary units and expands demand for cotton, chemicals, dyes, spinning mills, etc. These are considered as backward linkages. By increasing the supply of textiles, the textile unit facilitates the growth of ginning, spinning, machine-building and other units which is considered as forward linkage. These backward and forward linkages are very much required for the long- term vitality of every economy.

9. Dispersal by Economic Power

The modern world is dominated by economic power. Economic power is the natural outcome of industrial and business activity. Industrial development may lead to concerntration of economic power in few hands which results in the growth of the monopolies. The increasing number of entrepreneurs help in dispersal of economic power in few hands which result in the growth of monopolies. The increasing number of entrepreneurs help in dispersal of economic power into the hands of many efficient managers of new enterprises. Hence, setting up of a large number of enterprises helps in weakening the evil effects of monopolies.

Thus, the entrepreneurs are key to the creation of new enterprises that energises the economy and rejuvenates the established enterprises that make up the economic structure.

CHARACTERISTICS OF AN ENTREPRENEUR

Empirical literature analyses the characteristics of entrepreneurs, which found direct relationships between the need for achievement, locus of control and risk taking propensity with success in most cases. Again, the entrepreneurial characteristics required to launch a business successfully are often not those required for its growth and even more frequently not those required to manage it once it grows to considerable size. In otherwords, the role of the entrepreneur needs to change with the business cycle as it develops and grows.

An entrepreneur plays an important role in the development of an economy. He must possess some important qualities which are of great importance to the country's rate of economic growth. No two entrepreneurs are alike. In the words of Peter F. Drucker, a noted author, lecturer and consultant, some are eccentric, others painfully correct conformists, some are fat, some are lean; some are worriers, some relaxed, some drink heavily, others are total abstainers, some are men of great charm and warmth. Entrepreneurial qualities are in-born. However, some of the qualities can be enhanced by training and eperience. Robert D. Hisrich identifies adequate commitment, motivation and skills as some of the important qualities of an entrepreneur.

An entrepreneur should be one who bears, innovates or initiates and organizes the business. He is expected to combine all factors of production in a manner as to maximize output at minimum cost of production. Whether he performs the various functions effectively is determined by the nature of quality control, cost reduction, improved labour relations, profit earning, etc. All this is possible if the entrepreneur is especially a talented person and he possesses qualities like capacity to assume risk, technological knowledge, alertness to new opportunities, willingness to accept change and ability to initiate, ability to marshal resources and ability of organization and administration.

Professor David C. Mc Clelland of Harvard University found that entrepreneurs are likely to do well if they have the following traits:

Innovation Entrepreneurs are found to tackle the unknown. Entrepreneur is more than an inventor because, inventor only originates the invention, where as an entrepreneur goes much further by exploiting the invention commercially. Entrepreneurs deal with the changes. He does not continue with the old ideas.

Risk Taking Any new business poses risks for entrepreneurs. They may succeed or fail. They cannot foresee the way it will be. Entrepreneur takes risks. Successful entrepreneurs tend to launch ventures that fall between these two extremes, a middle ground in which the risk is neither too high nor too low. Moreover, and contrary to popular belief, entrepreneurs generally avoid ventures tht are pure gambles. They would rather depend on themselves than on luck.

Self-confidence Entrepreneurs believe in themselves. They firmly believe that they can beat any one in the field. They have the confidence that they can change the existing position.

Hard work Entrepreneurs are hard workers. Few people in our society work harder than entrepreneurs. Driven by their desire to excel, entrepreneurs put in longer hours of work.

Goal setting Entrepreneurs get happiness by setting and striving for goals. They may not always achieve those goals. What is more important for an entrepreneur is that of setting a meaningful goal. To entrepreneurs, merely choosing a new meaningful goal is self-renewing planning while carrying out the steps needed to reach their goal are stimulating. Reaching one goal set by entrepreneur will lead to the setting up of another goal.

Accountability Entrepreneurs take success or failure to their stride. Credit for success, blame for the failure will go to entrepreneurs. It is the profit that best tell entrepreneurs how well they are doing in the market. However, profits really serve only as a yardstick of performance, not as a goal.

However, various research studies reveal the following entrepreneurial characteristics:

- Capacity to assume risk
- Technical knowledge and willingness to change
- Total commitment.
- Drive to achieve and grow.
- Innovation
- Organisation abilities
- Motivation
- Taking initiative and personal responsibility
- Persistent problem-solving
- Seeking and using feedback
- Integrity and reliability
- Dynamism
- Aptitude
- Will power
- Creativity

- Self-confidence
- Self-control
- Realism and sense of humour
- Mental ability
- Business secrecy
- Human relations ability
- Effective communication
- Public relations
- High degree of ambition
- Flexibility and sociability
- Ability to marshal resources
- Will to prove superior to others

FUNCTIONS OF AN ENTREPRENEUR

The literature available on functions of an entrepreneur does not give full understanding of functions of an entrepreneur. Classical economists were of the view that entrepreneurs are the owners of the business to which they supplied the capital. They did not distinguish between capitalist and entrepreneur. But in modern corporation, ownership is separated from control wherein shareholders who bear the risk but do not exercise any control whereas board of directors of a small group of insiders bears little risk and receives a large remuneration even when no dividend is paid to the shareholders. Thus, the classical theory does not suit in the case of a large public company. Empirical literature analyses the characteristics of entrepreneurs, which found direct relationships between the need for achievement, locus of control and risk taking propensity with success in most cases. Again, the entrepreneurial characteristics required to launch a business successfully are often not those required for its growth and even more frequently not those required to manage it once it grows to considerable size. In other words, the role of the entrepreneur needs to change with the business cycle as it develops and grows.

Major functions of an entrepreneur may be recognizing the commercial viability of a product or service-formulating strategies for marketing, production, product development, etc. Peter Kilby identified some of the managerial functions of an entrepreneur. They are;

Exchange Functions

- Identifying marketing opportunities
- Gaining command over scarce resources
- Purchasing of Input
- Marketing of the products and facing the competition

Public Relations Functions

- Dealing with public bureaucracy
- Customer and supplier relation.
- Human resources management

Management and Control Functions

- Financial Management
- Production management (control by written records supervision and co-ordinating input flows with orders.)
- Factory control

Technological Function

- Industrial engineering

- Upgrading process and product quality

- Introducing new product techniques

Arthur H. Cole described an entrepreneur as a decision-maker and described the following functions of an entrepreneur;

i. Determination of objectives.

ii. Developmentof an organization.

iii. Securing of adequate financial resources

iv. Requisition of efficient technological equipment

v. Development of a market for the products, and

vi Maintenance of good public relations

Moreover, modern writers have emphasized that an entrepreneur is supposed to perform the following functions;

1. *Innovation* An improvement on an existing form or embodiment, composition or processes might be an invention, an innovation, both or neither if it is not substantial enough. Innovation means doing new things or the doing of things that are already being done in a new way. According to Schumpeter, the basic function of an entrepreneur is to innovate. Innovation includes production of new products, creation of new markets, introduction of new method of production, discovery of new and better channels of supply of raw materials and creation of new organizational structure. Innovation should be different from research and invention. Research gives us the knowledge, innovation results in the application of knowledge to produce the objects. Innovation is not based on research. Innovation can be completely independent of research. More

often innovations are not based on research but on ingenious combinations of existing materials and components.

Innovation is also different from invention as indicated separately in this book. Invention implies discovery of new ideas, new articles and new methods, where as innovation means the application of inventions and discovery to make new and desired products and services that can be successfully sold in the market. It is also not true that only big firms carry out innovations. Facts show that small and medium-sized firms due to their intensive flexibility can make a very significant contribution to technical development.

2. *Risk Bearing*   Due to unforeseen contingencies like changes in consumer tastes, techniques of production, government policies and new inventions, there may be losses which are borne by the entrepreneurs. Entrepreneurs in the game of business wherein risks and rewards are plenty will be ready to accept them. He is an enterprising person willing to assume the risk involved in inventions, new ventures and expansions. J.B. Say and others stressed risk taking as the specific function for the entrepreneur.

3. *Organisation and Management*   As rightly said by Alfred Marshal, organization and management of the enterprise is the main function of an entrepreneur. The entrepreneur has to decide the nature and type of goods and services to be produced. He brings together the various factors of production. Land, labour, capital are separately owned and scattered all over the world. It is the entrepreneur who brings them together and harnesses them to work in production. All in all he is a decision-maker. In order to minimize the losses, entrepreneur allocates resources more judiciously. He makes required alternation in the size of the business, its location, techniques of production, etc. Entrepreneur also undertakes the managerial functions like formulation of production plans, organization of sales and personnel management.

CONCLUSION

Entrepreneurs are, thus, the seeds of industrial development and the fruits of industrial development are greater employment opportunities to unemployed youth, increase in per capita income, higher standard of living, etc. In practice, entrepreneurs have historically altered the direction of national economies, industries, or markets. They have invented new products and developed organizations and the means of production to bring them to market. They have introduced quantum leaps in technology and more productive uses. They have forced the reallocation of resources away from existing users to new and more productive users.

The leadership, diligence, foresight and wisdom a great entrepreneur demonstrates has the potential to dramatically shape a nation's destiny. It is said that if India's richest 100 donated their fortunes the way Warren Buffet and Bill Gates did—over $250 billion—a quarter of the Indian GDP would be generated. But all said and done, the question of what the wealthiest Indians are giving now still remains a mystery. While most of them are not telling, and outsiders cannot pierce the veil, Yash Birla, the Scion of the Birla Empire is known in the industry as a true 'giver'. Yash says, "Keep in mind that there is always a higher purpose for your income", yet another philanthropist who would divulge just as much!

The Global Entrepreneurs (GE) International AS, Oslo has been set up in the year 2002 to help entrepreneurs make their dreams a reality. They provide assistance to individuals and firms those who want to start their own International

Business Consultancy. GE provides training to people those who want to shape their entrepreneurial skills, on completion of which the Company confers the Title of International Business Consultant (IBC). "IBCs are those who want to enter the international business arena. They are entrepreneurs who want to start business consultancy businesses using GE platform as a launchpad." IBCs also assist companies access international markets and in their internationalization process.

Carlos Slim Helu is a Mexican entrepreneur and businessman involved in a varied group of companies that include telecommunications, retail, banking and insurance, technology, and auto parts manufacturing businesses. He is the wealthiest Mexican man, the richest Latin American, and one of the top ten richest men in the world.

Carlos Slim Helú was born on the 28th of January, 1940 in Mexico City. His father Yusef Salim Haddad and mother Linda Helu were of Lebanese descent. Carlos was the 5th of six children. He studied engineering at the Universidad Nacional Autonoma de Mexico. The financial success that Slim Helu has achieved has been from finding undervalued companies and making them profitable. Telefonos de Mexico (Telmex) was acquired during a privatization period in 1990 of the Mexican government. Carlos was criticized for raising phone call costs soon after purchasing the business, but he went on to improve phone services in Mexico with the company offering local and long distance calls, mobile phone services, Internet services, and a telephone directory.

"It's not a question of arriving and putting in a whole new administration, but instead, arriving and "compacting" things as much as possible, reducing management layers. We want as few management layers as possible, so that executives are very close to the operations. We also don't believe in having big corporate infrastructures." Carlos Slim Helu. He has been referred to as the "Warren Buffett of Latin America", but he thinks of himself as an operator of companies, rather than just an investor (like Buffett).

Even though he has admitted to having very poor computer skills, he sees the Internet and technology as a major growth area in his group of businesses. He owns the largest Internet Service Provider (ISP) in Mexico and had one of the largest in the United States of America with his acquisition of Prodigy. Slim also owns the major computer retailer CompUSA, with more than 200 retail stores throughout the USA and Puerto Rico. As Helu rues, "Technology is going to transform people's lives and society everywhere in the world. My main task is to understand what's going on and try to see where we can fit in." However, in 2005 Forbes business magazine estimated Carlos Slim Helu's net worth to be $23.8 billion American dollars, making him the 4th richest person in the world. Also, in 2006, he was ranked as the third richest man in the world with an estimated $30 billion in assets. In 2007, the Mexican billionaire remained in third position but increased his wealth dramatically to an estimated $49 billion. Moreover, in June, 2007, it was reported that the wealth of Carlos Slim Helu increased to an estimated $67.8 billion, making him the richest man in the world. This puts Carlos Slim ahead of Warren Buffett and Bill Gates. Read more about Carlos Slim being the Richest Man in the World.

The Case of Shahid Balwa: From College Dropout to Billion Dollar Realtor

The 37-year-old Managing Director of a construction firm has indeed, stunned the real estate industry because of its meteoric rise in barely 5 years. "He is known to be careful for everyone's interest." The boy who grew up in a small family home near the landmark Maratha Mandir Cinema at Mumbai central and studied at Mazgaon's St. Mary School went on to become one of the wealthiest people in the world. Even The Forbes list has him as India's 66th richest man with with a net worth of $1.6 billion.

Hailing from the Chilya Sunni Muslim community, Balwa, who speaks immaculate Gujarati was dropped out of the college and entered the family's hotel business. His father Usman, started Balwa's restaurant at Marine's Lines and Balwa's hotel at Mumbai Central. However, in the late 1990s when the Balwas expanded, they sold their Mumbai Central house and bought a bunglow plot in Bandra. Later the profile of this business man shot to dizzying heights after he tied up with developer, Vinod Goenka to form DB Realty in the year 2006. In a few years, the construction company claimed to have 21 million square feet of saleable area in ongoing projects and another 40 million square feet in upcoming projects. In the year 2010, DB Realty won the right to redevelop the 100-acre Bandra (East) government colony alongwith Ackruti City, the Pune-based Kakade Infrastructure.

3

TYPES OF ENTREPRENEURS

Every economy is witnessed by the presence of a large number of entrepreneurs. They are also found in social and cultural activities. Entrepreneurs create great wealth not just for themselves, but for others as well. They also use the power of wealth, sometimes, to build sustained legacy for society at large. Behind the educational system of the United States is a huge amount of personal wealth donated by entrepreneurs. Without their support, some of the greatest initiatives to protect heritage, art and literature and environment would be difficult. However, entrepreneurs can be found among various sections of society, vis., farmers, artisans, workers, etc. In a study of American Agriculture, Danhof has classified entrepreneurs into four categories. They are:

i. Innovating entrepreneurs

ii. Adoptive or imitative entrepreneurs

iii. Fabian entrepreneurs, and

iv. Drone entrepreneurs

i. *Innovating Entrepreneurs* Schumpeter's entrepreneur was of this type. He introduces new products, new methods of production and opens new markets. These entrepreneurs are aggressive in nature. Innovating entrepreneur experiments and converts the attractive possibilities into practice.

ii. *Adoptive or Imitative Entrepreneur* Entrepreneurs of this type are found in underdeveloped countries. This type of entrepreneurs instead of innovating new things they just adopt the successful innovations innovated by others. However, some of the innovations made by others may not suit to the needs of underdeveloped countries. In such cases the imitative innovators may make some changes in the innovations made by the innovative entrepreneur so as to suit their requirements.

iii. *Fabian Entrepreneur* These entrepreneurs neither fall in innovative entrepreneur category nor in adoptive entrepreneur category. These are very cautious people. These entrepreneurs are rigid and fundamental in approach. They follow the footsteps of their successors. They are shy to introduce new methods and ideas. Fabian entrepreneurs are no risk takers.

iv. *Drone Entrepreneur* Fabian entrepreneurs are lazy in nature in adopting new methods, but Drone entrepreneurs are more rigid than Fabian entrepreneurs. They resist changes. They are laggards. They may close down their business but they do not accept for changes. Drone entrepreneurs refuse to adopt changes.

Other Categories of Entrepreneurs

Individual entrepreneurs These are found in small-scale business firms. When an individual sets up an enterprise, arranges finance, bears the risk and adopts the latest techniques in the business with an intention to earn profits, he is called as an individual entrepreneur.

Institutional Entrepreneurs In the case of business organizations where complex decisions are required to be taken, group entrepreneurs or institutional entrepreneurs emerge to arrange finance, bear the risk and adopt latest technological changes with an intention to earn profits.

Entrepreneurs by Inheritance This type of entrepreneurs are found in India, where a person inherits the business of the family through succession. They are also called as second generation entrepreneurs, since they inherit the family business firms and pass it from one generation to another.

Forced Entrepreneurs Circumstance force people to become entrepreneurs. Rich people from agricultural sector, unemployed youth, non-resident Indians may belong to this group. One finds more failure in this category because of not having proper training and understanding.

Business Entrepreneurs These entrepreneurs conceive an idea for a new product or service and then create a business (small or big) to materialize their idea into reality.

Trading Entrepreneurs These entrepreneurs identify market opportunities and stimulate demand for their products. They do not engage themselves in manufacturing activity. Trading may be national or international.

Industrial Entrepreneurs Industrial entrepreneur through research or otherwise estimates customer needs and wants and manufactures the products to cater to their needs. He is essentially a manufacturer.

Corporate Entrepreneurs   Corporate entrepreneur is one who promotes a corporation. A corporate undertaking is formed and registered under a statute which gives a separate legal entity. A corporate entrepreneur may engage either inbusiness or trade or in industrial activity.

Agricultural Entrepreneurs   Agriculture is considered as the backbone of our economy. Indian agriculture contributes approximately 17.5 per cent of the country's GDP. However, Agricultural entrepreneurs are normally engaged in the activity of raising crops and marketing crops, fertilizers and other inputs of agriculture. They are also engaged in allied agricultural activity.

A Case of Agriculture Entrepreneur

The idea of locally grown food is not new; however it is a growing movement that in the last 20 years has spawned a new type of niche market. Community Supported Agriculture (CSA) is a simple idea that creates rewards for both the farmer and the consumer by allowing consumers to buy local seasonal food that is delivered directly from the farm to the table.

Amber Springer and husband, Shanon, of rural Axtell, self described "foodies", have combined their knowledge of horticulture and food, creating a home-based business doing what they love, 6 Acre Wood CSA farm. Although both work full-time, Amber as a representative for Agency on Aging and Shanon as a food manager for the Kearney Housing Authority, the couple, their three children, Caleb, Maggie and Isaiah, and Amber's father Wendell Hansen, share responsibilities on the farm south of Axtell.

The CSA concept is simple. Typically, a farmer offers a certain number of "shares" to the public. A "share" buys a box of seasonal vegetables and/or fruit that is delivered weekly from the farm directly to the shareholder's home.

According to Local Harvest, a website devoted to locally grown organic food, tens of thousands of families have joined CSAs, and in some areas of the country there is more demand than there are CSA farms to fill it.

Amber Springer has discovered that even in central Nebraska, there is a market for 6 Acre Wood's bounty. "However, the idea for 6 acre of wood has always been in the

conversation," said Springer. "My husband and I talked about the concept for a long time when we were managing a vegetarian/vegan restaurant in Colorado. After we moved back to Nebraska to the family farmstead, my father, Wendell Hansen, started planting the cherry, peach, apple and almond trees and we began seriously pursuing the idea." As with all good things, it took time, nine years, for 6 Acre Wood to go from a concept to a reality. This is the pilot year for the CSA and the Springers are encouraged by the public's interest.

"We really thought we'd be doing good if we had one person sign up," said Springer. "We set a limit at five families, however we have more than that now. We have plans to expand the gardens if everything goes well this year." The gardens at 6 Acre Wood encompass approximately 2 acres, not including the fruit trees, strawberry, raspberry and blackberry beds. The variety of produce grown on the farm includes four varieties of green beans, beets, parsnips, okra, eggplant, 13 varieties of peppers, potatoes, sweet potatoes, onions, tomatoes, heirloom tomatoes, squash, cantaloupe, edamame (a type of soy bean), pumpkins and much more.

The Springer's use organic farming practices, meaning no pesticides, chemical fertilizers, or herbicides. Crop rotation and composting help ensure the health of the plants and the soil.

The members of the 6 Acre Wood CSA are guaranteed 6–10 different produce items delivered once a week for 15 weeks, beginning June 1 and running to September 15.The Springers harvest on Wednesday and deliver to members on Thursday morning. Members can also come to the farm on Sundays or Mondays to pick up produce. One of the important concepts of a CSA is the notion of shared risk. If a hailstorm wipes out all the peppers, the farmer and the consumers share the disappointment and hope the fall crops fair better. If there is a bumper crop of tomatoes, everyone shares in the bounty. That shared risk, says Local Harvest, is what creates a sense of community among the members and between members and the farmers.

The advantages for the farmer include receiving payment early in the season, which helps the cash flow and gives the farmer a chance to get to know the people who eat the food they grow. The advantages for the consumer are getting a weekly supply of fresh, organic vegetables and develop a relationship with the farmer who grows their food.

Pure Entrepreneurs   Pure entrepreneur is one who undertakes any activity to satisfy his ego. He is motivated to achieve or prove his excellence. He is status-conscious and wants recognition.

Induced/Motivated Entrepreneurs These are induced or motivated by Government or Non-Government agencies which may be providing financial and other assistance, concessions, subsidies, training, etc.

Spontaneous Entrepreneurs   Spontaneous entrepreneurs are in quite contrast with induced entrepreneurs. They commence their business out of their own confidence and talent. They are not induced by other agencies.

Technical Entrepreneurs   Technical entrepreneur is more of a producer rather than a marketer. They develop new/improved goods and services out of their specialization and skills.

Non-Technical Entrepreneurs These entrepreneurs are more concerned about developing alternative marketing and channels of distribution. They try to promote their business. Non-technical entrepreneurs are not concerned with the product development. Their target is not to change the production techniques but to increase the demand for the product by alternate course of actions.

Professional Entrepreneurs Professional entrepreneurs makes it as a profession in commencing a business. They develop a business and sell it to somebody and start another business only to sell it to others. They are not interested in managing or operating a business which is established by them.

First-generation Entrepreneurs These entrepreneurs do not possess any entrepreneurial background. They start an industrial unit by means of their own innovative sills.

Classical Entrepreneurs He is a stereotype entrepreneur whose main aim is to maximize his economic returns at a level consistent with the survival of the unit but with or without an element of growth.

Teentrepreneurs Entrepreneurs in their teens are called 'teentrepreneurs'. They are young, aggressive and supremely confident. They may not be able to hold a driving license but they are successfully juggling classrooms and board-rooms. They will never leave homes without ipods, laptops and blackberrys, which are like their extra limbs. The example of an illustrious teentrepreneur is found while citing various cases in the following section.

Other Entrepreneurs Entrepreneurs on the basis of gender and age may be classified as man entrepreneurs, woman entrepreneur, middle-aged entrepreneur, etc. According to area, entrepreneurs may be classified as urban and rural entrepreneurs. On the basis of scale of operation of the unit, entrepreneurs may be classified as large-scale industry entrepreneur, medium-scale industry entrepreneur, small-scale industry entrepreneur and tiny industry entrepreneur.

A Case of Business Entrepreneur

There was a time when Fiat and Ambassador ruled the roost. Not everyone has forgotten that vintage car. In place of a regular beetle shop business, two cousins have given a makeover to an old Fiat and turned into a shop. Their idea has attracted a large number of eyeballs and money. The two young minds hit upon the idea to redesign and spruce up an old, abandoned Fiat to set their business in motion. And the rest is history. Both the brothers have started

The Trahi Achyuta Bhramya Paan Shop. The shop has become the talk of the town, Bhubaneswar. It has been so popular that their idea was replicated by another businessman within a few months.

As opined by a customer, this shop is a stunner. Hundreds of people visited the shop on the very day it was started while another customer aptly speaks, "I have seen such a shop only on television." It was Ramesh, a taxi driver in Chennai and Mumbai, who broached the idea to Ashok. The latter used to run his business from a small cabin. The idea impressed him. According to the idea, the car was redesigned while removing the roof and rear doors in order to add multiple shelves. Given a fresh coat of paint the expenditure amounted to seventy thousands rupees.

Other than the customers, this unique model attracts curious on-lookers who are pusuaded to buy any item they like. The shop-on-wheels is a big advantage for the duo. Whenever Bhubaneswar Municipal authorities drive the cabins at unauthorized places, these innovative young entrepreneurs drive the vehicle to a safer place. However, the restricted space available in a Fiat while failing to accommodate two persons and a flourishing business in future, they would like to have a new and bigger mobile van for the purpose.

On May 18, 2007, Anshul Samar, CEO of Elementeo, clad in a white lab coat, found himself addressing a room teeming with 4000 executives. He had been invited to The Indus Entrepreneurs (TIE) conference—Tiecon 2007—in Santa Clara, USA. Sitting in the front row included Meg Whitman, President and CEO, eBay; Vinod Khosla, Founder, Khosla Ventures; Ravi Ventakesan, Chairman, Microsoft India and

Tim O'Reilly, Web 2.0 thinker. They were all ears as Samar, a 13-year-old entrepreneur and student of Sam H. Lawson Middle School in Cupertino, Santa Clara, spoke. Attendees agreed that there could not have been a better brand ambassador than Samar for the conference: He was "The New face of Entrepreneurship".

Recently, young haute couturier Pritam Panda has made the state of Odisha vis-a-vis India proud by bagging the World Chopard Young Entrepreneur Award (WCYEA), 2010 for art and design segment in the Global Award Ceremony in Dubai on 03.11.2010. He is the youngest from India and only designer from Odisha to have received the prestigious international award. However, his preceding winners of the award include Laksh Vaaman Shegal (Most Promising Entrepreneur), Gurubaksh Chahal (Entrepreneur of the Year), Vishal Gondal (Software Technology) and Padmaja Reddy (Woman Entrepreneur). WCYEA, the most recognized body for acknowledging the best entrepreneurs from the world, has quoted Pritam as the most challenging face in the field of promoting art and textiles. As Pritam (28) from Balesore in Odisha comments, "This is a huge encouragement for me that I have been successful in proving fashion as a serious business. My effort to promote the silk and weaving community in my own way has born fruits." At the same time, it is equally noteworthy that his creation has found a place in renowned fashin museum in Paris. He is the first Odia and the fourth Indian to receive this rare honour.

Pritam the 15-season-old designer has given about nine hits and four moderate seasons of his collections. He has ventured into diversified art and design options, some of which have received accolades worldwide.

ENTREPRENEUR AND INTRAPRENEUR

Entrepreneur is one, who commences his own business with his innovative ideas. He works for himself and for profits. Intrapreneurs are on the other hand work for entrepreneurs. The term "Intrapreneur" was put to use in America in the late seventies. In America, some of the business executives left their jobs and started their own small businesses because they were not given chance to test and implement their innovative ideas. Later this group achieved a phenomenal success in their new ventures. Like several such cases in India, these executives– turned-entrepreneurs posed threat to the organizations they left. Gifford Pinchot III, an American Management expert in his famous book "Intrapreneuring" used the word Intrapreneur for those who left their jobs and launched their own businesses.

Normally, ideas about new products and services come to the executives working in the organization. These persons have strong desire of personal achievement. If they are allowed to test and implement their new ideas in the organization, it will enable the organization to grow. Mr. Fenton, Founder and CEO of WorldBlu, Inc., a non-profit company specializing in organizational democracy feels that employees are more actively engaged in a company when they have a 'voice' in the decision-making process and feel that they matter as human beings, not just 'cogs ' in a corporate machine. We have moved from the 'industrial' age into the 'information' age and, with information now in the hands of masses, not just in the hands of elite, you have more power to the people, which has ushered in a democratic age. Secondly, democratic workplace is what Gen X and Y and knowledge workers, in particular want.

There should be a system and organization structure/ culture within a large organistion that would allow the executives to operate like entrepreneurs. The companies should provide enough opportunities, financial and technical assistance to intrapreneurs necessary for the developement and application of their ideas. Pinchot advocated for the creation of Intrapreneur status to a selected executives. The executives/ managers inside the organization should be encouraged to act as entrepreneur within the firm. But, in most of the cases, entrepreneurs like to run their own business rather than taking orders from others. In America, big corporation like International Business Machine (IBM), General Motors (GM) and Dupont are promoting intrapreneurs.

In India, Public Sector Undertakings (PSU) of state and central level are managed by bureaucrats not having any chance to entrepreneurship. This led to lack of enthusiasm among the executives which resulted in the closure of such undertakings. Of late, India Inc. is turning largely towards their employees for great ideas that could change the organization or process for the better. Providing the right platform for innovation is what many organizations concentrate on now. However, many firms today are fostering the spirit of innovation by leveraging employees' potential to ideate and collabarateively innovate. As experts say, "Such initiatives are bringing in a culture of creative thinking amongst employees and motivating them".

Both the entrepreneur and intrapreneur are innovators and both perform the functions of management. Yet they differ in the following ways;

Distinction between Entrepreneur and Intrapreneur

Entrepreneur	Intrapreneur
Entrepreneur is the owner of the business.	Intrapreneur works for the business.
Entrepreneur is independent.	Intrapreneur is semi-independent.
Entrepreneur raises the requisit capital himself.	Intrapreneur does not raise any capital.
Entrepreneur guarantees the money to suppliers.	No such gurantee is required to be given by the intrapreneurs.
Entrepreneur is one who bears full risks of his business.	Intrapreneur does not bear any risks of business.
Entrepreneurs operate from outside an organization.	Intrapreneur operates from within the organization. He is an organization man
Entrepreneur converts the ideas of intrapreneur into reality.	Intrapreneur creates new ideas.

According to Aruna Srinivasan, it is quite interesting to observe that, recently a trend opposite to intrapreneurship has also been observed. Most of the entrepreneurs are becoming intrapreneurs accepting executive posts in big companies who are lured by corporate pay and perks.

ENTREPRENEUR VS. PROFESSIONAL MANAGER

More often the terms entrepreneur and professional managers are used as synonyms. In the strict sense of the words they are different. Entrepreneurs are persons who initiate, organize, manage and control the affairs of a business unit that combines the factors of production to supply goods and services.

According to Sachar Committee on company law, a professional manager is an individual who

i. belongs to the profession of law, accountancy, medicine, engineering or architecture or

ii. is a member of a recognized professional body or

iii. is a holder of degree or diploma in management from any recognized university and possesses not less than five years of experience in an executive capacity in a company, corporation or in the government, or possesses minimum of ten years experience in the same capacity and in the same institutions mentioned in the third category.

A professional manager is one who specializes in the fields of planning, organising, directing, leading and controlling the efforts of others by the systematic knowledge.

A professional manager is required to have specific management knowledge. This may be with reference to technical process or human resources, administrative knowledge or legal and economic knowledge. Some of the entrepreneurs act as managers also, i.e., two in one. Normally a professional manager acquires knowledge through formal education, i.e., possessing of degree or diploma certificates. Some of the entrepreneurs may be self-made; without formal education they have become great entrepreneurs by virtue of their personal and cultural qualities.

Both the professional managers and entrepreneurs have similarities in their approach. They are equally responsible for results, they work with people, they follow sound principles like delegation of authority, responsibility, planning, etc., and they also take strategic decisions. However, an entrepreneur is different from a manager in the following cases:

Ownership   Entrepreneur is the owner of the business and self-employed whereas professional manager is a paid employee and not independent.

Innovation   Entrepreneur works to change in accordance with his personal vision. Entrepreneur innovates the things, changes the factor of production and thereby increases productivity and profit, whereas, professional manager deals with day to day affairs of a going concern. He keeps running a business on established lines.

Business   While an entrepreneur launches a new business, a manager operates an existing business.

Risk Bearing   Entrepreneur is a careful person. He takes a calculated risk and faces uncertainty whereas a manager does not share business risks. Manager is less tolerant of uncertainty of new venture.

Profit   Entrepreneur works for profits, often they are uncertain and even negative. But a manager on the contrary gets a fixed salary and can never be negative.

Qualification   Entrepreneur does not require any formal qualifications from any university or institution. One needs intuition, innovation, creative thinking,etc., whereas a manager needs to have basic academic qualifications.

Selected Cases of New Generation of Entrepreneurs

There are a few things which money cannot buy. For everything else, there is our card. A well known line from a credit card company's TV commercial. But that was a while ago. For high net worth Indians or anyone willing to spend between rupees two to five thousands a day for the service, there is a growing industry geared to get you the scarf that Brad Pitt wears or almost anything under the sun. The assisted services industry has come, of late to India. It was in October, 2010, Mumbai-based Kumud Khera started a company that assists working mothers. Khera offers the women wireless surveillance solutions in order to keep track of the servants and children. Such services have been available in the West for a long time because people live alone or in two's, have busy lives without anybody in the family to support. The rise of India's assited services industry is proof of its changing lifestyle. In the last two to three years, such a lifestyle has become quite common in India leading to a mushroom growth of such companies. As Khera claims there are almost 231 registered users for her company.

The money-rich-time-poor segment is proving to be rich in customers. Indian companies are busy offering personalized services and products. For instance, American express provides round the clock "concierge services" to the platinum card customers. This is an "invitation-only" service and customers are chosen after careful assessment of their monthly income and spending patterns. Membership comes at a price but members are not charged for services, including medical assistance, legal aid, emergency evacuation, locating and purchasing goods.

Born to a Govt. official in the year 1953, named Mr. Pillay gladly choose to make his career in the publishing industry. At the age of 32, Mr. Pillay set up his own publishing house called 'Pioneer Book Services' at Triplicane, Chennai with a small investment of ₹3000. However, in his late 40s, he took an adventurous step of undertaking book distribution throughout Tamilnadu and outside. The distribution business, Mr. Pillay made is in the name of an enterprise, Tamilnadu Book House at Chennai. Since, then he has not looked back. In order to put his business endeavour prominently, he established a new publishing house, named MJP Publishers in the year in the sole proprietorship mode. Notwithstanding the hurdles commonly faced while running a publishing house, Pillay has steered ahead always with a win–win situation. As he rues, "The most essential and the least wanted object of the present day, world is 'Book'." This, indeed, indicates his passion towards the publishing business. Being a New Gen Enterpreneur unlike his father, late Janarthanan in a white collar job, Mr. Pillay streadily runs his business till now.

Shailesh Baidwan, CEO of American Express Banking Corp in India says, sometimes they have received calls for matters as odd as monkey menace. He also recalls a customer asking "I want a Palestinian scarf like the one Yasser Arafat wears." And there was "Please deliver a hot and sour soup to my son in Cambridge." Also personal shopping services of such order are solicited for just a few thousand bucks.

Sahiba Walia lives in Delhi and works as a personal shopper. Because it has, of late, become greatly sought after due to Indians' increasing need for it at some point in their lives now. Walia receives ₹25000 for a 15 day package. However, she has started this two years ago following the personal shoppers she saw at work abroad. Furthermore, Delhi-based Subhra Benerjee says shopping related services are greatly in demand. For years, she helped friends and relatives buy and distribute festival gifts. This 2010, she made it a profession. She acknowledges happily the initial and positive responses from her customers, e.g., individuals and companies while offering to buy and distribute Diwali gifts. Banerjee charges roughly five to ten thousand rupees for her service while the costs of the gifts and commuting are charged extra.

Then followed Shopping Angels started by Bangalore-based Kaveri Sinhji just during the Puja. As she puts it, she heard about the personal shoppers available for ₹1000 per hour. She admits that she receives four requests from new customers everyday. However, those who have tried the assisted experience are not displeased. Sanjiv Samugam, Corporate Director of a Bangalore company says, "I found the shopping assistance experience an eye opener for bargains."

4

INNOVATION AND ENTREPRENEUR

INTRODUCTION

The slogan in the ever changing world of business is 'Innovate or Perish'. No organization can survive and thrive unless they continuously innovate products in view of the changing customer needs. Peter Drucker aptly puts it, "There are only two revenue centres in the company—marketing and innovation. All the other centres are those of costs." Sure, they are necessary. A company cannot move forward without them. But, marketing and innovation are 'critical'. No wonder, now so many companies are putting an emphasis on innovation.

One realizes that although we need far more innovation than we presently see, there are 'instinctively innovative' people across the world, who are involved with doing both complex and simple things. There are young people from the advanced countries like the US as well as from developing countries like India; and there must be many such all over the world.

Steve Jobs, the face of modern age innovation and cutting-edge design and technology once said, "Innovation distinguishes between a leader and a follower." Indeed, a small innovation spark in the prosaic darkness of indolence can light up the universe. Thus, the dearth of an innovative soul in an organization leaves the business and its employees inert and so, in order to avoid falling prey to such lethal 'innovation paralyses', engineering stalwarts today are taking that leap of faith into becoming serial jugaadus (innovative thinkers with bold moves who revolutionise industries).

Further, among the most frequently used words in LinkedIn, the internet community devoted to trading professional profiles for career advancement, is 'innovation'. In fact, it was, very recently, learnt at a glammy and educative gathering of social entrepreneurs—all happy to discuss their innovative approaches to connecting real world problems to real world profits. Then, it was not just the well meaning and ambitious professionals who are into the 'I' word. Whether it is car manufacturers advertising their newest model, politicians in search of a new mantra to sway their avid, hapless electorates, or governments projecting themselves as visionaries bustling into the future, innovation is the new holy grail. As put by various experts, "Such initiatives bring in a culture of creative thinking amongst employees and motivating them." A firm's Research and Development (R&D) is not the only source of innovations. Its whole value chain is the source of various kinds of innovations. The value chain is not the only source of innovations either. Suppliers, customers, competitors, related industries, public and private laboratories, universities, and other nations also constitute the sources.

For innovation to occur, something more than the generation of a creative idea or insight is required: the insight must be put into action to make a genuine difference, resulting for example in new or altered business processes within the organization, or changes in the products and services provided. We need also to move beyond our tendency to think of innovation as somehow oriented towards immediate, practical solutions. Indeed, we need to be little more innovative in how we identify innovation; so that we can recognise the inventiveness in, for instance, the creation of micro-insurance by organisations like SEWA or of policy innovations in some of the Indian provinces, whether concerning how to get children immunised at the school.

"Innovation, like many business functions, is a management process that requires specific tools, rules, and discipline." From this point of view emphasis is moved from the introduction of specific novel and useful ideas to the general organizational processes and procedures for generating, considering, and acting on such insights leading to significant organizational improvements in terms of improved or new business products, services, or internal processes. Through these varieties of viewpoints, creativity is typically seen as the basis for innovation, and innovation as the successful implementation of creative ideas within an organization. It should be noted, however, that the term 'innovation' is used by many authors rather interchangeably with the term 'creativity' when discussing individual and organizational creative activity. However, a convenient definition of innovation from an organizational perspective is given by Luecke and Katz (2003), who wrote: "Innovation is generally understood as the successful introduction of a new thing or method. Innovation is the embodiment, combination, or synthesis of knowledge in original, relevant, valued new products, processes, or services."

Here, in India we have seen an innovation revolution—at least rhetorically speaking. In case, you have not noticed, we are now something of an innovation society. We have seen the creation, in breathless sequence, of the National Innovation Foundation, the National Innovation Council, the launch of a national Innovation Initiative, Innovation Awards, and, of course, the National Innovation Act—designed to oversee the creation of special innovation parks, zones and presumably (though perhaps more elusively) minds. It is, however, true that the Indian experience shows some striking zones of achievement. The dense network of pharma research and labs in Hyderabad, Information Technology in Bangalore, as well as the space and nuclear sectors are all distinct examples of Indian innovation.

INVENTION AND INNOVATION

Innovation is different from invention. Invention implies discovery of new ideas, new products and new methods. The word entrepreneur is associated with innovation. Innovation should be different from research and invention. Research gives us the knowledge, innovation results in the application of knowledge to produce the objects. Innovation is not based on research, which can be completely independent of research. More often innovations are not based on research but on ingenious combinations of existing materials and components. Invention is the embodiment of something new. While both invention and innovation have "uniqueness" implications, innovation is related to acceptance in society (much like AIDS), profitability and market performance expectation.

Invention may facilitate innovations but invention is of little use to mankind unless it is put into commercial use. Thus, an invention becomes innovation only when it is embodied in a product or service that can be successfully marketed. In business, innovation can be easily distinguished from invention. Invention is the conversion of cash into ideas. Innovation is the conversion of ideas into cash. This is best described by comparing Thomas Edison with Nikola Tesla. Thomas Edison was an innovator because he made money from his ideas. Nikola Tesla was an inventor. Tesla spent money to create his inventions but was unable to monetize them. Innovators produce, market and profit from their innovations. Inventors may or may not profit from their work.

FORMS OF INNOVATION

Joseph Schumpeter defined economic innovation in "Theorie der Wirtschaftlichen Entwicklung" (1912). Schumpeter with his outstanding contribution to the literature of entrepreneurship says that an entrepreneur is basically an innovator as he introduces something new in the economy. He believes that entrepreneurship is essentially a creative activity. He is of the view that an entrepreneur does not only desire to raise his consumption standard through handsome profits but aspires to find a private dynasty also. According to him, an entrepreneur is one who innovates, raises money, collects inputs, organizes talent, provides leadership and sets the organization. Further, as emphasized by him, innovation can take any one of the following forms:

i. The introduction of new products with which consumers are not yet familiar or the introduction of a new variant of an existing product.

ii. The introduction of a new method of production that has not yet been tested by experience in the branch of concerned manufacturer.

iii. The opening of a new market, that is a market into which the new product has not yet entered, whether this market has existed before or not.

iv. The discovery of a new source of supply of raw material, irrespective of the fact as to whether that source already existed or it has been created now.

v. The carrying out of new organisation of any industry by creating of a monopoly or the breaking up of it.

Furthermore, Peter Drucker aptly puts, "Innovation is the specific tool of entrepreneurs, by which they exploit changes as an opportunity for a different business. It is capable of being presented as a discipline, capable of being learned and practised." However, systematic innovation consists in the meaningful and organised search for the changes and in a systematic analysis of the opportunities such changes might offer for economic and social innovation.

CONDITIONS FOR SUCCESSFUL INNOVATION

Drucker suggests three conditions for successful innovation which include;

1. Innovation at work. It requires knowledge and ingenuity. It makes great demands or diligence, persistence and commitment.

2. To succeed innovation must build on their strengths.

3. Innovation always has to be market-driven.

Moreover, Drucker has opined that an entrepreneur is one who always searches for change, responds to it and exploits it as an opportunity. Innovation is treated as an instrument of entrepreneurship. He has rightly defined an entrepreneur as 'One who always searches for change, responds to it and exploits it as an opportunity'. E.E. Hagen also has similar view while he defines entrepreneur as 'An economic man who tries to maximize profits by innovations. Innovations involve problem-solving and the entrepreneur gets satisfaction from using his capabilities in attacking problems'.

INVENTORS AND ENTREPRENEURS

Schumpeter, for the first time in 1934, assigned an important role of innovation to the entrepreneur. He did not equate entrepreneur with inventor. He also distinguishes between innovator and inventor. An inventor is an individual who creates something new for the first time, is a highly driven individual motivated by his own work and personal ideas. An inventor is highly creative with occupational experience that contribute to creative development and free thinking. Inventor is a problem-solver, has a very high level of self-confidence, is willing to take risks. He has the ability to tolerate ambiguity and uncertainity. An inventor is not likely to view monetary reward as a measure of success. The development of a new venture based on an inventor's work often requires the expertise. However, an entrepreneur, particularly innovating entrepreneurs are found in abundance in developed countries whereas there is dearth of these entrepreneurs in underdeveloped countries. A country with little or no industrial tradition can hardly produce innovating entrepreneurs. Such entrepreneurs can emerge and work only when a certain level of development is already achieved and people look forward to change and progress. Innovating entrepreneurs have played a major role in the rise of capitalism, through their enterprising spirit, urge to do something different, hope of making money and ability to identify and exploit opportunities.

TYPES OF INNOVATION

According to Kuratko, Donald F. and Richard M. Hodgetts, innovation can be of the following types:

1. **Innovation** It is the production of totally new product or service or process not yet tried.

2. **Extension** It involves new use or application of an already existing product, service.

3. **Duplication** It is the replication of an already existing product, service or process.

4. **Synthesis** It is the combination of existing concepts and ideas in order to form a new application.

SOURCES OF INNOVATION

Innovations resulting from a spark of genius, are a result of conscious, purposeful and committed search for opportunities which may exist in the internal and external environment of an enterprise. Kuratko Donald F. and Richard M. Hodgettss have underlined the following internal and external areas of opportunities.

1. **Unexpected Occurrences** Sometimes unexpected success or failure pose to be a major reason of surprise for the enterprise. They are not usually anticipated. Peter F. Drucker remarks, "These unexpected successes and failures are such productive source of innovation opportunities, because most business undertakings discard them".

2. **Incongruities** These occur whenever a gap arises between the expectation and the reality. The gap, however, motivates the entrepreneur to innovate.

3. **Process Needs** These needs are created whenever situation demands for innovation. Entrepreneurs are prompted to innovate to satisfy the required process need.

4. **Industry and Market Changes** Changes in consumer tastes, fashions, likings and disliking, and technological advancement result in change in the structure and design of the product. These changes make room for tremendous opportunities for innovations and improvements.

5. **Demographic Changes** Demographic changes create entrepreneurial opportunities. For example, fast food concept sufaced fast in order to cater to the requirements of employed and young people.

6. **Perceptional Changes** It is reflected in the change in the people's attitude, feelings, etc. Change in perception does not change the object or the fact, but changes their meaning or attitude in that regard.

7. **Knowledge-based Concept** These are the basis for the development and creation of new products and markets. These are time-consuming as they need testing and modification, sometimes improvement.

Training meeting about sustainable design The photo shows a training meeting with factory workers in a stainless steel ecodesign company from Rio de Janeiro.

The work force is a very important source of innovation. There are several sources of innovation. The traditionally recognized source is *manufacturer innovation*. This is where an agent (person or business) innovates in order to sell the innovation. Another source of innovation, only now becoming widely recognized, is *end-user innovation*. This is where an agent (person or company) develops an innovation for their own (personal or in-house) use as existing products fail to meet their needs.

The Case of Marketing Innovation

Taher Abbasi, co-founder and CEO, Cellworks group Inc., aptly puts, "There are many untapped territories and fundamental ideas waiting to be explored. The foundations of start-ups are built on the very concept of innovation and exploration of the same. The willingness of such industries to survive and grow in today's tough market through innovation gives them an edge over the rest. They are focused on project execution and deliverables and are equipped with an urge to excel despite being a small fish in a big pond."

In an age, where trendy young people, who are as accustomed on to the latest i-pod as they are to yoga, are sporting Kolhapuri chappals with jeans being traditional, yet modern seems to be the new norm in marketing. Building on conventional behavioural trends of Indian consumers, such as eating food with hands, stocking savouries in large ceramic jars and sipping tea in steel glasses, markets are unleashing point of purchase (POP) innovations to provide a multi-sensory experience to their customers.

Leading modern retailer, Future Group that launched its private brand "Tasty Treat" soup with a mug in the year 2009, ran the promotion three times over during the year to grow the category. Although, table manners specify that soup must be

---

served in a bowl, Future Group decided to offer soup in mugs, an idea the consumer was more at ease with. The POP scheme was based on the inferences drawn from a research conducted by the group among 100 consumers in five cities to understand soup consumption habits. The finding of the Group was that 32 per cent among the soup consumers were infrequent as it required a formal atmosphere (read: having soup from a bowl with a spoon). However, a majority of consumers, 70 per cent indicated that it is convenient for them to have soup in a mug at home. This insight prompted the Future Group to break away from Western Tradition and offer mugs along with Tasty treat soups to trigger more volumes.

"It was important to take soup to the masses. As a retailer, we are in direct contact with consumers. It is our responsibility to drive consumption through differentiated offerings. We suggested a change in the way customers have soup from formal (bowl and spoon) to casual (mugs). Today, Tasty Treat, has 25 per cent share of the soup category in our stores," said Devendra Chawla, business head (Private Brands), Future Group. Moreover, the Group realised that a bowl would require an additional investment by the consumer, while mugs are readily available at homes. Similarly, when Britannia industries started offering biscuits in jars, it realised it had moved closer to the Indian consumers, who were traditionally stocking eatables like cookies in large wooden jars at home.

Rogers and Shoemaker have summarised their findings concerning the attributes of innovator which include:

(i)   More educated.

(ii) Higher in social standing.

(iii) Less dogmatic.

(iv) More emphatic.

(v) Better equipped to deal with abstraction.

(vi) More receptive to risk in general.

(vii) Higher in achievement motivation.

(viii) Higher in social participation.

(ix) More cosmopolitan.

(x) More often engaged in interpersonal communication.

(xi) A more active information seeker.

(xii) More knowledgeable about innovations.

(xiii) An opinion leader.

(xiv) More in contact with persons outside the social system.

Some thinkers believe that innovations can be carried out only by big business houses. Their opinion is based on the assumption that big business houses have adequate financial resources, and managerial skills. In reality, most of the innovations are atributted to small-scale businesses. It is due to their in-built flexibility, small firms can respond to new demands without any loss of time and can easily exploit new ideas. A large firm operating under the constraint of size and competition tend to achieve perfection in order to survive and increase profits. Small firms, on the other hand, can adjust promptly as per requirement and can exploit the opportunities as and when they are available. Also, as opposed to large organizations, start-ups do not consist of more than 20 to 30 employees, hence, work is performed like a close-knit family. "Rearing various innovations and addressing several issues together while increasing their scope to grow as a single organization come among the major driving forces of working in a start-up" remarks Shriram Adu Koorie, co-founder, Asklaila, an information search service.

Market Outcome

According to Paul H. Wilken, various types of changes initiated by entrepreneur are:

1. **Initial Expansion**   Original production of goods.

2. **Subsequent Expansion**   Subsequent changes in the amount of goods produced.

3. **Factors Innovation**   Increase in the supply or productivity of factors.

   (a) **Financial**   Procurement of capital from new source or in new form.

   (b) **Labour**   Procurement of labour from new source or new type, upgrading of existing labour

   (c) **Material**   Procurement of old material from new source or use of new material.

4. **Production Innovations**   Changes in production process.

   (a) **Technological**   Use of new production process.

   (b) **Organisational**   Change of form or structure of relationship among people.

According to Albert Einstein, "You cannot solve a problem on the same level that it was created. You have to rise above it to the next level." The example of Toyota may be rightly put here: Toyota aims to realize a tomorrow where people, society and the earth, can coexist in harmony. To this end, it is constantly working towards optimizing the energies of people and technology, through its array of world class cars.

Innovative products are engines to growth and profitability and hence, academicians and practitioners have developed an interest in product innovation.

5. **Market Innovations**   Changes in size or composition of the market.

Innovation is also studied by economists in a variety of other contexts, for example in theories of entrepreneurship or in Paul Romer's New Growth Theory. In network theory, innovation can be seen as "a new element introduced in the network which changes, even if momentarily, the costs of transactions between at least two actors, elements or nodes, in the network". Market outcome from innovation can be studied from different lenses.

Many a times, however, business managers are setting product affordability as a primary attention for new product development and innovation research activities. "The largest market opportunity lies at the bottom of the pyramid. Products that have traditionally focused on select segments need to cater to specialized features that may not have mass appeal, and often become too expensive. Such a product ends up at the stratosphere of the market and eventually gets forced out." says Suneet Singh Tuli, CEO, Datawind Ltd.

Innovation by businesses is achieved in many ways, with much attention now given to formal research and development or "breakthrough innovations." But innovations may be developed by less formal on-the-job modifications of practice, through exchange and combination of professional experience and by many other routes. The more radical and revolutionary innovations tend to emerge from R&D, while more incremental innovations may emerge from practice, but there are many exceptions to each of these trends. Furthermore, recent theoretical work also speak different stories. Empirical work shows that innovation does not just happen within the industrial supply-side or as a result of the articulation of user demand, but through a complex set of processes that links many different players together—not only developers and users, but a wide variety of intermediary organisations such as consultancies, standards bodies, etc. However, work on social networks suggests that much of the most successful innovation occurs at the boundaries of organisations and industries where the problems and needs of users, and the potential of technologies can be linked together in a creative process.

Mark Zuckerberg, the founder of facebook, the youngest billionaire in the world at 26 has never cared about making money when he founded facebook. His main urge was to do something innovative, entrepreneurial and most importantly, cool. Six years ago, Mark started Facebook from his college dorm. Today, the privately held company could be worth $50 billion (₹220,000 crores) and and an American movie made on him is pathbreaking in that it is about talent, made by talented people and for a country that celebrates talent. For, only in the USA, can a boy in his 20s, coming from nowhere, create a company worth billions in six years.

There is a story of 18-year-old Masha Nazeem living in a small town in Tamil Nadu. She saw her father melting red lac over a naked flame. Considering it dangerous, she developed a contraption to heat the lac without a flame and pour it on the envelope so that the seal can now be pressed over it. She now has a patent on the 'flameless seal maker'. Having done this, she looked at the needs of the elderly at the railway platforms (her own experience in Japan, where she jugged a suitcase everywhere without any help). She developed a luggage carrier on wheels, where the suit-case can be lifted to the level of the compartment floor and the bags rolled into the compartment without the need to carry them. She has patented this 'mechanical porter'. Masha has 8 innovations to her credit so far including a burglar alarm and a conveyor belt system.

Madam Curie, the famed scientist was once invited to inaugurate a large, new, well-equipped research centre in France. When she saw the luxurious building, she was viably upset. She was asked, whether, she was not happy to see such a state of the art facilities, at last, for the promotion of Science? Her reply was simple, "To do great research, you do not need grandiose buildings with well laid out gardens. You need creativity, passion, hard work and the human spirit and of course, some necessary equipments and facilities." This young girl, Masha seems to prove Madam Curie right in her perspective of 'innovation'.

Interestingly, a list of the twenty largest countries (as measured by GDP) by the International Innovation Index is available below:

Rank	Country	Overall	Innovation Inputs	Innovation Performance
1	South Korea	2.26	1.75	2.55
2	United States	1.80	1.28	2.16
3	Japan	1.79	1.16	2.25
4	Sweden	1.64	1.25	1.88
5	Netherlands	1.55	1.40	1.55
6	Canada	1.42	1.39	1.32

Rank	Country	Overall	Innovation Inputs	Innovation Performance
7	United Kingdom	1.42	1.33	1.37
8	Germany	1.12	1.05	1.09
9	France	1.12	1.17	0.96
10	Australia	1.02	0.89	1.05
11	Spain	0.93	0.83	0.95
12	Belgium	0.86	0.85	0.79
13	China	0.73	0.07	1.32
14	Italy	0.21	0.16	0.24
15	India	0.06	0.14	−0.02
16	Russia	−0.09	−0.02	−0.16
17	Mexico	−0.16	0.11	−0.42
18	Turkey	−0.21	0.15	−0.55
19	Indonesia	−0.57	−0.63	−0.46
20	Brazil	−0.59	−0.62	−0.51

Technological Innovations

No organization can survive and thrive unless they continuously innovate keeping in view the changing customer needs. In recent years, technological innovations have emerged as an important source of competitive strength, and firms in many industries have achieved success by competing through innovation. Innovation literature while rich in typologies and descriptions of innovation dynamics is mostly technology focused. Most research on innovation has been devoted to the process (technological) of innovation, or has otherwise taken a how to (innovate) approach.

Conclusion

Entrepreneurs, for the sake of their survival, have to keep track of the emerging trends and innovate. Innovations result from conscious, deliberate and purposeful search for new opportunities. These innovations are specific, clear and designed applications of products targeted at creation of new customers and new markets. Moreover, It is widely accepted that innovation is the key to success for any organisation and to stay ahead in the competition, firms need to innovate constantly. Hence, many firms today are fostering the spirit of innovation by leveraging employees' potential to ideate and collaboratively innovate.

Case Study

Practically, one may be able to wear silk saree, dhoti and shirt spun not out of a silkworm thread, but from the banana plant with the help of a banana thread separator. The separator invented by K. Murgan, a mechanical engineer from Tuticorin got patented in July, 2011 and took its shape after 40 unsuccessful attempts. According to Murgan, the stem of the banana plant has 15 layers, with the outermost used for tying garlands. The other 14 layers can be used for silk production. The fibre equals the silkworm silk in lustre and tension strength. The separator machine can process 60 lakh banana plants per year while two sarees can be spun using banana fibres from a single tree. It would be very eco-friendly and adaptable as well to natural dyes.

At the same time, it is highly noteworthy that the decade beginning with 2011 made a brilliant and useful revelation in respect of automobile technology. The innovative development can check drivers for alchohol content. Located in contact points across a car, this measures the alchohol its driver has consumed. The vehicle goes into 'lock-down' mode if this quantity is found to cross a legal limit. Indeed, the innovation comes as a breath of fresh air. However, due to a steep rise in the quantity of fatal accidents occurring as a result of "intoxicated driving", this novel technology will undoubtedly enhance our quality of life. This car can evaluate a driver's capacity, compelling the intoxicated to take alternative transport or sleep it off. In this way, the accidents are curtailed and those on a high can enjoy without worrying about navigation or police checks. Additionally, this car can neither be bribed nor cajoled proving itself to be an admirable gadget.

Innovators as Socially Relevant Individuals: Selected Illustrations

When R. K. Pandey boarded a low-cost airline for an emergency board meeting, to his amazement he found a bartanwali seated next to him asking for in how many minutes the 'gaddi' would stop at the Bangalore airport. Though the naive question brought smile to his lips, amazement was writ large on his face. "An airborne housemaid?" Has the common Indian's lifestyle changed so? Cocooned in his CEO forums and an affluent lifestyle, Pandey may have missed the social revolution, but for the millions who are enjoying the fruit of an undying passion of a few 'lifestyle changers', this is a far-fetched dream come true.

When it comes to lifestyle, we do not mean the guy who brought Armani or caviar to the so-called Swish set that comprises a minuscule population. Here we mean a few good men who dared to revolutionise lifestyle for the 'real' India. Their vision permeated and trickled down the lowest denominator. Harbingers of hope, they taught millions the true meaning of the word 'aspire', for example, Ratan Tata and his People's Car, Nano. The ₹ 1 lakh car today has given shape to an autorickshaw driver's dream of owning a car. Similarly, it was the vision of an ex-army captain Gopi Nath to give wings to a billion hungry passengers that gave birth to Air Deccan. The man has to be credited for kick-starting the revolution in the Indian skies.

Not too long ago, it was just temples that could have been considered as classless destinations in the country. But a man called Kishore Biyani changed it all. With Big Bazaar, he gave Indians not only the taste of shopping in air-conditioned environment but also a classless destination called 'malls' where the Mercedes owner as well as its driver shop side by side. What is it that puts an Anil Ambani, who revolutionised the Telecom Sector, by bringing mobile phones within the reach of majority of Indians?

Tusi Tanti

Every Evangelical has a story about the moment he first glimpsed his destiny. Tanti has two. The first came with his electicity bill, back in1995. The young engineer's fledgling textile company, Suzlon, was just starting to take off. His new line of polyster yarns was doing well, but India's shaky power grid and the rising cost of electricity offset any profits."We were constantly innovating, yet we were not able to control the price of power". Tanti, then 49 decided to generate his own. After a few years of research, he settled on wind power, buying two turbines to provide his energy needs. The initial cost was steep. But the company with its headquarter in Pune was no longer buffeted by the seesawing cost of fossil fuels. Soon Tanti was preaching to fellow industrialists about the economic advantages of staying off the grid.

Epiphany No.2: In early 2000, the inveterate traveller read report on global warming predicting that without a radical decrease in the world's carbon emissions, some of his favourite tourist destinations, including the Maldives, would be under water by 2050. It was then that Tanti realized his fate lay far beyond the latest advances in synthetic fibres."I had a very clear vision", he says. "If Indians start consuming power like the Americans, the world will run out of resources. Either you stop India developing, or you find some alternate solution."

If wind was the answer to Suzlon's energy needs, asked Tanti, then why could not it fuel the growth of other industries? By 2001, Suzlon had sold off its textile manufacturing and plunged into the relatively new field of wind turbine generators. Later, with factories on four continents and wind farms across Asia, Suzlon proved to be the fourth largest wind turbine maker in to the world. In the wake of oil pricing hovering over more than a hundred dollars a barrel, Tanti was all the more confident that wind would be the energy of the future, and that Suzlon would help launch the industry into the mainstream. As aptly commented by Tanti, "green business is good business." But it is not just about making money. It is being about being responsible. Suzlon's main factory at Pondicherry runs exclusively on wind power. Rain water is collected to tend the lush ground, and factory construction disturbed not a single tree.

A Case at HCL

The innovation cell at HCL Technologies is called 'Value creation'. 'Value portal' is a corporate-wide initiative designed to encourage, facilitate, manage and document innovations at HCL. The value creation ideas are logged in the value portal and empowers the employee to think on innovative lines and generate value-added ideas. At a global level, SAP Labs India too has specific programmes (like Global Business Incubator), which scout for ideas from employees and work on them in conjunction with employees to productise the ideas.

Mitticool Refrigerator and Non-Stick Clay Tawa

Mr. Mansukhbhai R. Prajapati, 39 years of age, is a craftsman from Wankaner, near Rajkot in Gujurat. He belongs to a family of potters and teracotta craftsmen and has used his expertise to create two very interesting innovations—a Mitticool refrigerator and a non-stick clay tawa. These are products which have become part and parcel of most urban households, but Mansukhbhai's innovation is helping to bring them into a poor man's household as well.

Non-Stick Clay Tawa

Mansukhbhai got the idea for making this tawa while working at a tile-making factory. Here, he used to work at a process which could churn out hundreds of tiles in a day. He thought of producing the tradtional handmade earthen pan (locally called kaladi or tavdi) in a smilar vein. But there were no presses or suitable machines for mass production of tawas. He decided to build the machine himself. In due course, he developed his own tawa-making press by redesigning old tile presses. These could produce more than 700 tawas a day. This was a seven-fold increase in productivity compared to making 100 tawas by hand each day.

Encouraged by his peers, Mansukhbhai started experimenting with the constituents of the tawa. His goal was to create a new material mix that would make the tawa unbreakable and give it enhanced durability and finish. It took him almost a decade of trial and error to get the mix right. Business picked up very slowly, and his first real break was an order for 3000 tawas from a trader in Bhuj. This order became regular, while other orders trickled in. So far, Mansukhbhai has sold over 30,000 tawas. His tawa is a substitute for the more expensive Teflon coated metal non-stick tawas with the added advantage of giving better taste to the food cooked in it. It is basically a clay tawa with Teflon coating. While his existing setup can manufacture 1000 pans per day, his next innovation was the earthenware refrigerator, the design of which he perfected by 2005. The zero cost novel fridge turned out to be a contemporary product appealing to budget conscious rural customers as well as new age customers looking for eco-friendly energy efficient options. The earthenware refrigerator has a height of 18.5 inches and width of 11 inches weighing 20 kgs. With, however, two larger water tanks at the top and bottom, it is similar to the working of clay pots that keeps water cool in summer. Available for less than ₹2500, the prototype made people sit up and take notice. A civil engineer by profession, Mr. V.V. Patel got higly impressed by its potential and placed an order for 100 pieces. Keeping the Mitticool refrigerator in a proper ventilated place allows better evaporation, in turn enhancing its performance. Besides, this product with zero cost of electricity preserves the original taste of fruits and vegetables.

Mitticool started to receive coverage in the local media. The promising product was scouted by Gujrat Grassroots Innovation Augmentation Network (GIAN). Mansukhbhai's innovations have receieved appreciation and acclaim from various quarters including Discovery, Aaj tak, New Delhi TV, BBC, etc. Being in a hurry to cross new frontiers with his Mitticool fridge, he wants to improve his product and build an advanced model fitted with a Reverse Osmosis (RO) unit.

SUGGESTED READINGS

1. Ettlie, John E. (2006). *Managing Innovation* (2nd ed.). Butterworth-Heineman, an imprint of Elsevier.

2. Evangelista, Rinaldo (2000). "Sectoral patterns of technological change in services, economics of innovation". *Economics of Innovation and New Technology.* 9:183–221.

3. Fagerberg, Jan (2004). "Innovation: A Guide to the Literature". In Fagerberg, Jan, David C. Mowery and Richard R. Nelson. *The Oxford Handbook of Innovations.* Oxford University Press.

4. Hitcher, Waldo (2006). *Innovation Paradigm Replaced.* Wiley. *Innovation.* Boston, MA: Harvard Business School Press.

5. Mansfield, Edwin (1985). "How Rapidly Does New Industrial Technology Leak Out?". *Journal of Industrial Economics* (The Journal of Industrial Economics, Vol. 34, No. 2) 34 (2): 217–223.

6. Miles, Ian (2004). "Innovation in Services". In Fagerberg, Jan, David C. Mowery and Richard R. Nelson. *The Oxford*

Handbook of Innovations. Oxford University Press. pp. 433–458.

7. *Paradigm Replaced*. Wiley. *Innovation*. *Boston*, MA: Harvard Business School Press.

8. Schumpeter Joseph (1934). *The Theory of Economic Development*. Cambridge, MA: Harvard University Press.

9. Scotchmer, Suzanne (2004). *Innovation and Incentives*. Cambridge, MA: MIT Press. Silvestre, Bruno dos Santos; Dalcol, Paulo Roberto Tavares. "Geographical proximity and innovation: Evidences from the Campos Basin oil & gas industrial agglomeration—Brazil". *Technovation* (Elsevier) 29 (8): 546–561.

5

WOMEN ENTREPRENEUR

INTRODUCTION

"Empowerment is all about letting go so that others can get going."
Even though women constiute almost half of the total world
population, historically women have palyed a disproportionately
small role in the field of business. Entrepreneurial development
to a large extent depends upon the economic, social, religious,
cultural, legal and psychological factors prevailing in the
society. In a male dominated society women have been victims
of social prejudices and discrimination. Parents prefer male
child to female. Women are considered to be weak, passive and
dependent on others. Women are not exposed to risks which
adversely affected on their self-confidence, innovativeness and
risk taking ability. In traditional society, women are confined to
four walls. But, in advanced countries like USA, UK, Canada,

France, Australia and Germany, women entrepreneur account for not less than one-third of the small businesses especially in the areas like retail trades and hotels making a significant impact on all segments of economy.

DEFINITION

Woman entrepreneur according to Governemnt of India is an entrepreneur who runs an enterprise owned and contolled by her and having minimum financial interest up to 51 per cent of the capital and giving at least 51 per cent of the employment to women. Thus, woman entrepreneur is one who intitiates, organizes and operates a business enterprise. In developing countries like India, such innovators are found less in number when compared with advanced countries.

WOMEN AND ENTREPRENEURSHIP

Commercialisation and modernization of the economy gradually eliminated many of the avenues of employment to women in agriculture and industries and thus enabled them to find ways of supplementing their family income. As a result of this a section of urban women have emerged as potential entrepreneurs. This development is of significant importance in the society. It is since the last decade that the women have started emerging on the business scene and some of them have achieved remarkable success too. Some of the successful women entrepreneurs in India are Smt. Vimala Pitre—manufacturer of surgical equipment, Smt. Manik Vanrekar of Leather crafts, Smt. Radhanika Pradhan of Plastic industries and Smt. Gogate for Drugs, etc.

REASONS FOR WOMEN ENTREPRENEURSHIP

One must accept the fact that entrepreneurship is not related to sex of an individual. Women can be as successful entrepreneurs as man. The entry of women in business is obviously a recent development in the orthodox, traditional, social and cultural environment of our society. Our society has not allowed women to think independently in the past. But in the last decade, economic compulsions have led more and more young girls to take up employment and potential source of women entrepreneurship has emerged. The following are some of the reasons for emerging women entrepreneurship.

- Not finding a job.
- Unable to work in her house.
- New challenges and opportunities for self-fulfillment.
- Proving their innovate skills.
- Need for additional income.

The above reasons clearly indicate that economic compulsions, family responsibilities and desire to enjoy social status compel the women to take up enterprises.

WOMEN ENTREPRENEURSHIP IN INDIA

As far as India is concerned, women constitute a very negligible proportion of the total entrepreneurs. Women in India are still shy and emotionally attached to family. Majority of women entrepreneurs are engaged in the unorganized sector like agriculture, agro-based industries, handicrafts, handlooms, kitchen activities (pickles, powders and papads) and other cottage-based industries like basket making, etc. In 1990s women in India constituted 46.5% per cent of total population of which only 4.5% women account for total self-employed in India. With the spread of education and awareness among women, women entrepreneurs have entered into engineering, electronics, energy, ready-made garments, printing fabrics, eatables, doll making, poultry, plastic, textile designing, dairy, canning, knitting, etc.

As per 1991 census, only 1,85,900 women entrepreneurs were recorded. During 1995–96 there were more than 2,95,680 women entrepreneurs. During the Eighth five year plan, the number of women enrepreneurs is expected to rise up to 5 lakhs with the rise of mahila sanghams and governmental assistance. Several government organizations are providing Entrepreneurial Development Programmes (EDPs) through training. National Institute of Entrepreneurship and Small Business Development, New Delhi is an apex body for training and research in entrepreneurship. National Rural Employment Programme (NREP), Integrated Rural Development Programme (IRDP), Rural Landless Employment Guarantee programme (RLEGP) are some of the other schemes under which women and rural entrepreneurs are getting training assistance.

Our late Prime Minister Mrs. Indira Gandhi stressed that women have trailed behind men in almost all sectors and their status could be raised by generating opportunities for their independent means of employment. Consequently reorientation of government policies and programmes were initiated for accomplishing more effective economic growth by enhancing women's productive roles. Sixth five year plan, for the first time, introduced a special chapter on "Women and Development". During the last three decades various studies have been undertaken to identify the real issues confronting women. A number of working groups, task forces and national conference were organized to discuss the issues of women entrepreneurs. In addition, a Women Welfare Development Bureau was also set up.

WOMEN ENTREPRENEURS—PROBLEMS

Most of the women entrepreneurs face peculiar problems like illiteracy, fear of risk, lack of training and experience, feeling of insecurity, limited purchasing power and competition from male entrepreneurs. A most important problem faced by women entrepreneurs is that they do not get enough support from family members. Women in rural areas suffer more when compared to urban women entrepreneurs. In rural areas joint family system is still the norm. Women in a family are considered as helpers. Some of the major problems faced by women entrepreneurs are as under.

Paucity of Funds   Most of the women are dependent firstly on parents and thereafter on their husband and children. They fail to get external funds due to absence of tangible security and credit in the market. In most of the cases properties are not registered in the name of women. Banks do not encourage women entrepreneurs. Women entrepreneurs to the large extent depend on personal saving and loans from friends. This has resulted in the failure of women entrerprises.

Competition   Women entrepreneurs face severe competition from large-sized organizations and male entrepreneurs.

Middlemen   Middlemen exploit women entrepreneurs than men entrepreneurs because marketing involves a lot of running which is a tough task for women. Thus, for marketing their products women entrepreneurs are heavily dependent on middlemen who pocket large amount of profit.

Legal Formalities   Women entrepreneurs find it extremely difficult in complying with various legal formalities in obtaining licences, etc.

Procurement of Raw Material   Procurement of raw materials is really a tough task for women entrepreneurs. This may result in high cost of production.

Travelling   Women entrepreneurs cannot travel from one place to another as freely as men do. Women have some peculiar problems like staying out in the nights, distant places, etc., which deter the marketing opportunities.

Family bond Women are understood to be emotionally attached to their families. They are supposed to look after the children, husband and other family members. Women entrepreneurs' success largely depend upon how much support they get from their family members. A woman has to strike a balance between business and her family. Recently the advent of kindergartens, creches, family planning, etc., has helped the women to squeeze leisure time that can be fruitfully used in running the family business.

Traditions and Customs Most of the Indian women suffer from traditions and customs which discriminate women from men. Women are not allowed to venture out by husband and other elderly persons in the family. Women are considered to be helpers of the family. Especially in rural areas women suffer from traditions and customs. The potential of women are not properly utilized.

Risk Bearing Women entrepreneurs have less risk bearing capacity, because they lead a protected life. Lack of training, illiteracy, late start, etc., are the other problems that deter the growth of women entrepreneurship. In addition, a variety of personal, social, economic, legal, resource and support system constraints restrict women entrepreneurs in achieving their enterprise targets. Efforts to identify these hurdles and carving their remedial strategies would go a long way. Further, effectiveness of the communication in every network is very essential because the women do not have access to scientific information, latest know-how and supporting agencies, etc.

Remedies for the Problems of Women Entrepreneurs

Once an enterprise starts, the difference between a male and a female must be forgotten because an entrepreneur is an entrepreneur, business is business and profit and loss strictly depend upon entrepreneurial competencies. In order to make the women entrepreneurs to start the business venture, the following measures may be adopted.

i. *Creation of Finance Cells* The financial institutions and banks which provide finances to entrepreneurs must create special cells for providing easy finance to women entrepreneurs. For the conveniences of such entrepreneurs, these cells should be manned by women staff members.

ii. *Concessional Rates of Interest* The women entrepreneurs should be provided finance at concessional rates of interest and at easy repayment basis. The cumbersome formalities should be avoided in sanctioning the loans to women entrepreneurs.

iii. *Proper Supply of Raw Materials* Women entrepreneurs should be ensured of proper supply of scarce raw materials on priority basis. A subsidy may also be offered to make the products manufactured by women entrepreneurs cost competitive and reasonable.

iv. *Changing the social attitudes* It is absolutely necessary to change the negative social attitudes towards women. The elders, particularly mothers and mother-in-law, need to be made aware of the potentiality of the girls and their role in the family and society. Unless the social attitudes are made positive through education and awareness programmes, the women entrepreneurs cannot get the required support from their family members.

v. Offering Training Facilities   Training is essential for the development of entrepreneurship. It enables the women entrepreneurs to undertake the venture successfully as it imparts required skills to run the enterprise. Additional facilities like stipend, good hygienic creches, transport facilities, etc., can be offered to attract more and more women entrepreneurs. Presently, the economically weaker entrepreneurs of the society are offered such training facility under Prime Minister's Rozgar Yojana (PMRY) programme. FICCI, Lions Clubs, Rotary Clubs and other voluntary organizations can also arrange such training programmes for women.

vi. Setting up Marketing co-operatives   Proper encouragement and assistance should be provided to women entrepreneurs for setting up marketing co-operatives. These co-operatives shall help in getting the inputs at reasonable rate and they are helpful in selling their products at remunerative prices. Hence, middlemen can be avoided and women entrepreneurs derive the benefits of enterprise.

Thus, proper education, comprehensive training, setting up of separate financial institutions, development of marketing co-operatives to a large extent help to flourish the women entrepreneurship in India. Further, both government and non-government agencies should play an important role.

Selected Cases of Indian Women Making A Global Mark

They are the grand dames of their domain, conquering home ground as well as making an impact on the international stage. The original trailblazers, they have paved the path for women who have tried to make a mark in the western world. Here one finds five formidable women entrepreneurs sharing their success mantra and the secret behind that fire in the belly.

I. Poonam Soni

She changed the mindset of the Indian buyer from buying jewellery as an investment to buying it as a work of art. From high-end stores in Paris to New York, she has wowed the glam world with her exotic creations.

Her Struggle   In the late 80's, when everything from clothes to hair was getting fashionable, jewellery was neglected. No one dared take the risk of giving it designer status or experiment on the look. Her first line of jewellery collections, inspired from the carvings on the Sistine Chapel in Rome, got her an offer from Harrods as early as 1992. For he, life itself is learning. The downs taught her humility and the ups made her ambitious. As she aptly puts, " The power is within me to shape my life. I have a strong conviction that if I do not get something I desire, something bigger awaits me". She does not compete with Indian or any Western competitor. She creates her own space and revels in it.

II. Adarsh Gill

She showcased her first collection in New York in the late 70s and graced the front page of New York Times. From First Ladies to coy brides, she has dressed up fashionistas in her now famous embellished georgette saris and gowns.

The Struggle; She only remembers her success and even today she can proudly say, "I am the only Indian designer who got a half page cover in New York Times in the late 70s. When I presented my first collection in late 70s, a top-notch American buyer told me that she did not want to do business with Indians. She slammed the phone only to call me a few minutes later apologizing!". As she rightly emphasizes, "Success mantra has to be hard work and consistency. For me, the learning graph never ends. I remember this beautiful outfit I had designed for the wife of a theatre-owner. She called after mid-night to say that the outfit was very heavy yet the praises made it worth wearing. Moments like these humble me." Gill remembers to have been inspired by Jacqueline Kennedy for her fashion sense. She was among her first clients at Saks Fifth Avenue.

III. Anu Malhotra

She produced one of the first travel shows for television, 'namaste india'. She showcased her documentaries in various global film fests, including the Miami Film Festival and Cannes.

The Struggle: She started making travel shows for television in the 90s. I learnt on the job. As a woman, I had to prove myself doubly hard, even to my cameraman! As she recollects, "In 2000, I visited a remote village in Kinnaur for their annual puja. I realized that it was inner peace that mattered." At the Miami Film Festival, she commanded a standing ovation. She believes that respect cannot be demanded, it can only be commanded.

IV. Ritu Dalmia

From taking Indian Cuisine in London out of curry houses to fine diners, to being knighted with the order of the Star of Italian Solidarity, she has proved that food is the great leveller. Ritu had three failed restaurants to prove what struggle means! In 1993, Delhi was not ready for a fine diner, then in the late 90s, she tried her best to shift Indian food in London from curry houses to fine, elegant restaurants. The Eureka moment in her life was the day she decided to quit her father's company and open her own restaurant. As she puts herself, "I have been a hands-on person. In Vama, London, I have cleaned toilets and dried glasses".

A pat on the back, in India or abroad is encouraging. India right now is the best place for a restaurateur; globally the competition is very tough! As she further adds, "A woman she admires is Rose Gray, the owner of River café in London and New York. She expired in 2009. Rose proved that you do not need to be an Italian to cook Italian food wonderfully.

V. Shahnaz Husain

From Harrods in London, Bloomingdales in New york, to Seibu in Japan, Shahnaz has lifted the curtain of mist and antiquity from India's herbal heritage, earning the sobriquet of India's beauty ambassador. About her struggle, she says, "I was a given a counter at the Festival of India in London in 1980. I sold India's ancient civilization in a jar without financial resource and advertising. It was a matter of great pride and honour for me when I was invited by the US president Mr. Obama to represent India for the US Presidential Summit on Entrepreneurship held in 2010. I was also invited by Harvard University to speak on how I created a brand without publicity."

Her success mantra: The desire to exce, courage, relentless determination to succeed and the ability to work hard are necessary ingredients for success. Create a demand for your product. I believe a satisfied client is your best advertisement. You may start in a small way but you have to think big.

Global Milestones: The international milestones are recognition of her efforts to spread ayurveda. India will lead the int'l cosmetic industry in the 21st century. As her source of inspiration, she says, "No other woman has fascinated a generation of Indians the way Indira Gandhi has. She had courage, dignity and poise in the face of great odds. What amazed me was her abilty to remember the smallest details about people, their likes and dislikes.

VI. Shika Sharma

In corporate circles, Shikha Sharma is known as a strategic thinker. Her bold move to acquire one of India's best known investment banking firms—Enam—will help Axis Bank gain a foothold in the fiercely competitive sector and enable it to become an integrated financial services firm. The deal comes at a time when the government is planning to sell equity in about 60 state-run firms and therefore shows Sharma's immense foresight. Although government offers do not bring in much money but that takes the merchant bankers higher up the M&A league table.

According to well-known sources of analysts, the deal brings enormous value to Axis Bank as also for Enam. At present, in India, like in other parts of the developed markets, Merger & Acquisiton (M&A) deals need the backing of a strong balance sheet. On its part, Axis Bank has been growing at about 20–30 per cent annually, without the help of a strong investment banking segment. Now with a strong M&A advisory and equity issuance issue teams under her command and a strong balance sheet to back a deal that Enam brings to the table, Sharma would probably like to grow the Bank at a much faster pace. Also, personally it may be viewed as Sharma's hunger to prove a point after she left ICICI. Professionally, it also strengthens the invest banking division of Axis Bank considerably.

CONCLUSION

Today, it is crystal clear that the contemporary world needs greater participation of the women in any socio-economic field, more so, in a field like entrepreneurship. Women are transforming not only the social face of a nation–state, but also its economic vigour. In addition to their social role, they are increasingly becoming active participants in the economic mainstream. Before we conclude, we make this point more clear with the facts given below.

Very recently, stalls were put up at Public Information Campaign site at Ramtek organized by the Ministry of Information and Broadcasting to showcase the developmental schemes being executed under the Bharat Nirman. An entrepreneur named Karuna was present among scores of Bharat Nirman beneficiaries of various central schemes being implemented either through the State Government or by the apex bodies of the concerned Union Ministries. From Nagardhan, another small town near Nagpur she had sold all the leather bags she brought to this three-day Fair for display within the first few hours of the beginning of the Fair. Now she was doing brisk business in bags made of tarpaulin or other materials.

Karuna Ananta Paunikar, very confidently insisted on using her full name when told that she would be written about. She is a member of Rani Laxmi Mahila Bachat Gut of Nagardhan, a group formed under the Swarna Jayanti Gram Swarozgaar Yojna which is an integrated programme for self-employment of the rural poor with the objective of bringing the poor families above the poverty line by organising them into Self Help Groups (SHGs). Karuna got to know about the scheme through the 'Sahyogini' of the Panchayat Samiti Nanda

Khadse who encouraged her to join the self-help group and start her own enterprise. A diffident Karuna, on much prodding by her mentor, took a small loan of ₹10,000 and started making small items like washing powder, phenyl, etc. Soon she realized the potential of her small enterprise and expanded her product range by taking an additional loan of ₹60,000. She set up a small unit for making a variety of bags and now employs eight to ten women on contractual basis to make bags and other products. Though she had her husband by her side at the stall, it was clearly Karuna who was calling the shots.

However, another participant Renuka Bidkar is very different from Ashok Chawade and Karuna Ananta Paunikar. 39-year old Renuka is a post-polio paralysis affected person and needs a wheel-chair to move. But she did not allow her disability to deter her in any way, rather it steeled her resolve to accept bigger challenges in life and succeed in business. She took a small loan from the National Handicapped Financial Development Corporation (NHFDC) and started making candles, incense sticks (Aggarbattis), chalk, liquid soap, soft toys, etc. Soon, Renuka repaid the loan and expanded her enterprise by deploying more people and producing a bigger range of items. She makes it a point to give employment to people with disabilities in her enterprise as far as possible. Renuka now also runs an organization which works for the upliftment of persons with disabilities and helps them getting jobs or mentors them for taking up self-employment. "Now the larger objective of my life is to help and guide those persons with disabilities who do not have means and resources to meet their basic needs and they need jobs to lead a dignified life", Renuka says with a sense of conviction.

6

RURAL ENTREPRENEURSHIP

INTRODUCTION

Rural entrepreneurship is defined in broader sense "as the enthusiastic willingness of a villager to organize his/her economic activity, whatever it may be (a business, a job, an investment, etc.), with the help of appropriate technology and practices conceived for a sustainable living. It is difficult for the rural mass to be entrepreneurs without getting support from another individual, body or corporate. The single option available to handle this issue is to effect desired transformation in the form of a business model that would interest the rural participants and the participating external bodies or corporates. According to Krishnan and Jegadeesan, the model should be profitable and replicable. Further, the new innovative business model will form the life blood of the rural economy. In this context, Mary Paulseel puts appropriately, "Not only do these businesses create new local jobs, but also generate new growth and wealth in their communities. Entrepreneurs use regional assets to build their companies and they are critical in getting new ideas and commercialise the same. They are, by and large, responsible for the quality of life we all enjoy."

Although agriculture today still provides income to rural communities, rural development is increasingly linked to enterprise development. Since national economies are more and more globalised and competition is intensifying at an unprecedented pace, affecting not only industry but any economic activity including agriculture, it is not surprising that rural entrepreneurship is gaining momentum as a force of economic change if many rural communities are to survive.

Rural entrepreneurship has an important role to play in the development of Indian economy. In view of the fact that 70 per cent of the country's population live in villages, adequate funding and support can provide a thriving entrepreneur atmosphere for these communities. So far, it is known that rural India in contrast to its counterpart is economically poor, younger, more isolated geographically, isolated from the main markets, culturally embedded in traditions, less dynamic economically and experiencing depopulation. Moreover, rural India lags behind in terms of experiencing the burgeoning economic growth. While addressing at the 30th convocation of the Orissa University of Agriculture and Technology in October 2010, the Vice-President of India has rightly pointed out that the last six decades have witnessed the dramatic transformation of Indian agriculture from "shortages to surpluses". This has happened simultaneously with a decrease in the share of agriculture in the GDP from over 50 per cent at the time of Independence to around 15 per cent today. He also has remarked that trends of the last 15 years are a cause of concern. After improving steadily from 1980 to 1997, the terms of trade turned against agriculture since 1999. However, to check the trend, Mr. Ansari stated that the 11th Five Year plan had suggested measures for a "more efficient, sustainable and inclusive growth" in Indian agriculture. These measures also address the "technology fatigue", "sustainability question" and "yield gap", with a sharp focus on rain-fed areas and 85 per cent of farmers who are small and marginal farmers.

Here, it may not be out of place to mention that India is not a country of more than a billion hungry people, it is a country of more than a billion consumers. The Indian rural market with its huge population base—approximately three times of its urban counterpart—has a huge opportunity to explore. The increasing affluence, supported by favourable monsoons and good agricultural output results in a good boost to the rural economy being transformed as a large customer base for the corporates.

In the earlier years, rural India was a taboo for marketers. Now, the scenario has completely changed. It has now become their buzzword. Many successful corporate organizations including Crompton Greaves are already set to open new exclusive outlets with customized products for village and rural markets. Rural India is no longer a segment that is largely illiterate, naïve, poor and agrarian. Monsoon no longer largely influences the buying habits of rural population. In the seminar, "The Challenges of Rural Marketing in the 21st Century", the Head of MART, the specialist in rural marketing and Rural Development Consultancy said (2004) that 50 per cent BSNL mobile connections were attributed to small towns and villages.

An increase in literacy rates, siginificant contribution by the non-farm sector in the rural income and the penetration of media are catalyzing the growth of consumerism in the minds of rural people.

Mahatma Gandhi in his historic remark once said that "the poor of the world cannot be helped by mass production but only by production by masses". Indian policy makers have been always guided by this since the time of independence. Whether it is rural entrepreneurship or urban it has always given the way to employment opportunities. Entrepreneurship has fairly been recognized as the backbone of every region of the country. While 70 per cent of Indians live in rural areas, limited land availability has failed to adequately absorb labour in agriculture. Moreover, many farming entrepreneurs work hard throughout the year while they are not yet able to rise above the poverty line. Thus, it clearly points out the need to develop industrialization, lest rural migration to urban areas will continue and rural unemployment shall remain a nagging problem. However, rural industrialization has not taken off very far despite adequate attention given to it by the policy makers since independence. Thereby, there arises an urgent need to create additional employment in rural areas. Entrepreneurship, in fact, gives the right answer to address such a grave problem.

DEFINITION

Simply stated, rural entrepreneurship implies entrepreneurship emerging in rural areas or rural entrepreneurship meaning rural industrialization. Industrialisation cannot sustain without entrepreneurship whether rural or urban. So, it can be said that entrepreneurship precedes industrialization. Rural entrepreneurship is the only solution to rural poverty and backwardness. Rural industries are generally associated with agriculture. As defined by Khadi and Village Industries Commission, "Village industry or a rural industry means industry located in rural areas, population of which is not more than 100000 or such figure which produces goods or render any services with or without use of power and in which fixed capital investment per artisan or a worker does not go beyond ₹1000". As per the modified definition, an industry located in rural area, village or town with a population of 20000 and below and an investment of 1 lakh rupees (in plant and machinery, land and building) is classified as village industry. The limit to raise the ceiling of capital investment upto 1 lakh rupees was introduced through the KVIC (Amendment) Bill, 2004 in the Lok Sabha. This results in increase in the number of village industries eligible for assistance by the KVIC.

FEATURES OF VILLAGE INDUSTRY

Agriculture and rural development are the mainstay of India's growth strategy. Rural industrialization is generally viewed as a group of traditional industries like handloom, Khadi, handicraft, sericulture and coir. All these are classified as rural industries although some of them are located in urban areas as well. An industry with the following features can be considered as a rural industry:

1. Very low investment;
2. Low gestation period;
3. Decentralised production system;
4. Products are either essential mass consumer goods or handicrafts;
5. Use of locally available raw material (in a few cases);
6. Cater to limited markets;

7. Product popularity in foreign markets for unique nature and aesthetic values.

TYPES OF RURAL INDUSTRIES

Although entrepreneurial competencies remain the same, rural entrepreneurs differ from urban entrepreneurs in terms of attitude, aspirations and objectives because of the difference in environment. As they have a low capital assets base, they usually avoid more risk and seek to realize the tangible results of their entrepreneurial initiatives within a very short period. However, they can be classified into the following categories:

i. Farm Entrepreneurs

They are such persons chiefly engaged in farming. Agriculture is their main source of earning. As agriculture is the mainstay of Indian economy, it provides food to millions and raw material for our industries. Agriculture is no longer practiced by rule of thumb. Work in agricultural sectors ranges from the totally academic pursuits of research to commercial activities of establishing farms, plantations, orchards, and carrying on exports of produce from them.

Moreover, without any land holding of their own, people are willing to stay in villages and aid in agriculture.

Agriculture is the mainstay of a state like Odisha in the eastern part of India. Mayurbhanj in Odisha happens to be a tribal district. The foundation crop of Mayurbhanj, millet, better known as 'Kheli', has been able to bring smile on the faces of the farmers of the district who reaped a bumper harvest during the cropping season in the year, 2010. As Jadunath Baskey, a tribal farmer aptly puts, "In the month of June, he had sown 1.5 kilogram millet seeds across nearly half an acre of his land and he harvested 213 kilogram of millet during the early part of September".

Baskey, who was strongly opposed to the use of genetically-modified seeds had attended Kishan Swaraj Yatra. He said that the farmers were opposed to the cost-intensive, profitless, modern and chemical farming that would spoil their self-reliant, sustainable agricultural system. "With only two cart load of farmyard cowdung compost, I could reap a bumper harvest from millet this year", Baskey said and added that this millet was nutritious and healthy because it was grown traditionally. According to Marandi, an agricultural executive of a Mayurbhanj-based NGO, "These farmers are strong champions of the old-fashioned agricultural system and they know the techniques of maintaining the local biodiversity." As he further puts, "Farmer through his years of experience in traditional farming ends up becoming an agronomist, breeder, a plant pathologist, a horticulturist, a seed technologist and a nematologist, all rolled into one".

Like Baskey, there are 2000 farmers who are organized under the aegis of Mayurbhanj Paramparik Krushak Sangathan who have taken a vow to conserve the local biodiversity through strict traditional agricultural methods and never allowing BT seeds to sneak into their farm lands.

ii. Artisan Entrepreneurs

They are the people possessing skills such as masonary, blacksmithy, carpentary, pumpset repairing, board painter, art, etc. Such skill can be inherited and refined through professional training.

iii. Merchants and Traders

It includes businessmen who deal in goods required by local villagers and the neighbouring people. They can either produce the goods or act as the middlemen.

iv. Tribal Entrepreneurs

Originally, they belong to various tribal communities. Also they operate predominantly in tribal villages.

ROLE OF RURAL ENTREPRENEURS

Rural entrepreneurship development is a complex phenomenon needing the attention of social, political and economic institutions. Its role can be discussed as under:

i. *To provide employment* Rural Entrepreneurship is labour-intensive. It gives a clear solution to the ever increasing unemployment problem. Rural industrialisation has a high potential for generation of employment and income as well.

ii. *To check rural exodus* Rural entrepreneurship can bridge the gap between the income of rural people and that of the urbanites. It also helps build strong infrastructure base like power, road, bridge, etc. Rural migration can be reduced through rural entrepreneurship.

iii. *To balance regional growth* Rural entrepreneurship can reduce concentration of industrial units in urban areas encouraging balanced regional development.

iv. *To promote artistic activities* The age-old rich heritage of rural India is preserved through protection of art and handicraft through rural entrepreneurship.

v. *To reduce on social evils* Rural entrepreneurship development can effectively address the issues such as poverty, growth of slums, pollution in cities, etc.

vi. *To awaken the rural youth* Young minds in rural areas are prompted to embrace entrepreneurship as a career.

vii. *To improve standard of living* Rural entrepreneurship also increases the literacy rate of rural population. Their education and self-employment will prosper the community thus increasing their standard of living.

PROBLEMS IN GROWTH OF RURAL ENTREPRENEURS

Rural entrepreneurship faces various problems such as fear of risk, illiteracy, lack of training and experience, limited purchasing power and competition from urban entrepreneurs. For better understanding these problems can be enumerated as follows:

i. **Paucity of Funds** Rural entrepreneurship fails to attract external funds due to absence of tangible security and credit availability. The procedure to get loan facility is too time consuming so as to discourage the rural entrepreneurs.

ii. **Competition** Large-size organizations and urban entrepreneurs pose a serious threat to rural entrepreneurship. They face high input cost associated with increased cost of production.

iii. **Legal Formalities** Such formalities and their adherence pose problems in a rural situation.

TRADITIONAL INDUSTRIES

The growth and performance of traditional industries are as follows:

Khadi and Village Industries (KVIs)

KVI has been instrumental in generating large-scale employment, particularly in rural areas with low capital investment and short gestation period. The handloom sector provides direct and indirect employment in weaving and allied activities. This sector has been able to withstand competition with the help of various development and welfare schemes of the government including schemes of financial assistance. It contributes to almost a fifth of cloth production in the country with substantial contribution to export earnings.

Case of Agro/Rural Entrepreneurship in Odisha

A villager in Sonepur district, Sarat Narayan Mohanty, aged 35 started off with 100 saplings, which he procured from the department of horticulture. In the year 2007, his business has grown so much that he presently produces 2000 roses everyday. As Mohanty recalls, "My love for the flower bloomed when I was in school, I would steal roses from the school garden and keep them near my head when I went to bed." After he became a youngman, he tried his hand at various jobs and business ventures but none could satisfy him. Finally, the rose won over his heart which helped him fetch a steady income.

He has already sold over one lakh saplings in the year 2009–10. As reported by him, he possesses expertise in four varieties which is sold like hot cakes. While his monthly turnover touches nearly one lakh rupees whereas he invests nearly forty thousand rupees. Sarat also says that he availed a loan amounting to 18 lakh rupees from the Department of

Horticulture with 50 per cent of subsidy. According to him, the demand for rose is growing for which he desires to expand his business further. Rose vendors from Bolangir, Sonepur, Boudh and Kalahandi are making a beeline to collect flower from his nursery. Sarat has plans to open outlets in these places for better supply and speedier realization of the returns from his business. As the Government officials remark, Mohanty would get more support once he gets a grade as per norms. "Presently, there is a limited scope for him. After his product gets graded as per the guidelines, the loan availability will increase. In fact, the nursery developed by Mohanty is a rarity and considered a model enterprise.

A Case of Rural Livelihoods and Women in Gurgaon

Harnessing Value (HarVa) BPO was started near Gurgaon at a time when the economic downturn in developed economies pushed mighty corporate to bankruptcy. Consequently, there was increasing need for value creation and cost efficiency. In a landscape, that is known for its cultural rigidity and male-dominant social order, married women are being trained and hired for jobs that require them to move out of their houses and deal with large database for domestic and international clients alike. According to Ajay Chaturvedi, founder of HarVa, the organization is also experimenting with community farming, career guidance for the rural youth, and micro finance. Further, it has been able to motivate farmers to integrate their lands and grow lemon grass, which is a natural replenishment for soil that has lost its nutrients due to heavy use of pesticides and fertilizers. Besides, an acre of land normally owned by a farmer proves it insufficient to grow such crops. HarVa plays a catalatic role to organize the farmers in order to pool 70–80 acres of land. It also has helped the farmers set up an oil extracting plant with an initial investment of ₹30 lakhs.

Truly speaking, in villages around Gurgaon, computers and cow dung have been equally important for the rural BPO executives. These women executives, many of whom were semi-illiterate till a few months ago, are balancing the two contrasting sides of life quite well. Following the socio-capitalistic model of business, the organization believes that inflated prices for the most basic commodities do not have a future. As rightly, it is said, "charity is passé". No government or individual can change the rural economy by pumping in cash because development is nothing but a byproduct of increased productivity. The BPO in the case gets the women in the villages to work for it because they stay for it for long and combating attrition in BPOs results in a considerable amount of money saved.

7

TOURISM ENTREPRENEURSHIP

INTRODUCTION

We have already made a rich discussion in the foregoing chapters on a multi-faceted entrepreneurship and its contribution to a nation's economic development. Understandably, the economy of a region significantly depends upon its entrepreneurial potential. Given its natural, physical and financial resources, it can develop in a sustainable manner when there is rational and optimal use of such resources. Needless to say, tourism being a popular global leisure activity proves to be a positive instrument towards poverty reduction, creating job opportunities and contributing to social harmony. Sustainable tourism development is most conducive for a sound and relevant society. The tourist product availability is, however, the prerequisite for any organisation's marketing function. In the case of tourism product, the basic raw materials include a country's natural beauty, climate, history, culture, and the people. Other aspects would be the existing facilities necessary for comfortable living such as water supply, electricity, roads, transport, communication and other essentials. In other words, tourist product can be seen as a composite product as the sum total of a country's tourist attractions, transport, accommodation and of entertainment which leads to the consumer satisfaction. Thus, the tourist product can be very much a man-made one or nature's creation improved upon by man. Each of these components of a tourist product is supplied by individual providers of services like hotel, airlines or other suppliers, and is offered directly to the tourists by them. This, undoubtedly, provides lot of scope for entrepreneurship in tourism sector.

Tourism Perspectives and the Policy Presciptions

The World Tourism Organization defines tourists as people who "travel to and stay in places outside their usual environment for more than twenty-four (24) hours and not more than one consecutive year for leisure, business and other purposes not related to the exercise of an activity remunerated from within the place visited". By now, tourism has emerged as the number one largest smokeless industry in the world. Considered as the most rapidly expanding industry across the world, tourism business has proved to be profitable with no obvious constraints to its growth, few barriers of entry and few effective regulatory provisions to take the environment into consideration. At the same time, the unscrupulous entrepreneurs and sometimes mindless government agencies have explored tourism potentials causing impendiments to the environment, people or a community. This degeneration in vulnerable and humanistic industry called for an alternative tourism so as to preserve and protect the sector for the posterity. Thus, with a paradigm shift, from mass tourism to sustainable tourism, eco-tourism has assumed popularity for last couple of decades. Being nature-based, eco-tourism implies education and interpretation of the natural environment and is managed to be sustainable from ecology point of view. Its definition centre round three important aspects, such as nature, tourism and community. Being in tandem with this modern approach to the field of tourism, The Federation of Indian Chambers of Commerce and Industry have begun promoting a comparatively new concept, i.e., rural tourism in India and abroad. Eco, Green and Rural tourism are very much interrelated. Rural tourism enterprises are community based. It encompasses all the activities that cater to national and international tourists through facilities that are owned, managed and serviced by the members of the village community and run essentially as a community based initiative (Khannka and Bhuyan, 2004).

In India, however, the industry received the status of industry in the VIIth Five Year plan, while the Xth Plan identified it as one of the major sources for generating sustainable livelihoods and employment. This industry is witnessing a strong period of growth, driven by coordinated government campaigns to promote 'incredible India' and growth in high spending foreign tourists. India is a treasure trove for tourism development. In the words of the former President of Indian democracy, Dr.APJ Abdul Kalam remarked in the inauguration of the Fifth Global Travel and Tourism Summit in New Delhi in April, 2005: "Today, the Indian economy depends a lot upon its invisibles and the tourism sector is a major part of it". Travel and tourism economy is contributing close to 5.5 per cent to the total GDP and 5.4 per cent to the employment. It is one of the prime foreign exchange providers to the Indian economy. The fact remains that for a country like India bursting with tourism opportunities, we have been slow on the uptake in promotion of tourist destinations. For instance, hardly the governments in states and the centre put the desired emphasis on the beaches in contrast to the Thai Government at Bangkok. However, in view of the mobilie nature of the tourists, tourism entrepreneurship needs to take care of the consumer's (i.e., tourist) taste, temperament, life and living. It goes without saying that an alert entrepreneur cannot afford to neglect or under-estimate these aspects.

The first National Policy on Tourism was announced in the year, 1982 in order to collate the discrete efforts made during the early years of Indian Planning. It was by 1986, tourism was accorded the status of an industry. Later, the National Tourism Policy, 2002 has focussed on seven broad objectives, viz., Welcome, Information, Facilitation, Security, Co-operation, Infrastructure Development, and Cleaniliness. Against this backdrop, activities like drug trafficking, wildlife hunting, flesh trading are viewed illicit and illegal in India.

ENTREPRENEURSHIP IN TOURISM

Entrepreneurship in tourism, due to its specialized nature refers to the activities primarily designed for the effective and profitable interaction of demand for and supply of tourism products. While it includes all forms of activities associated with a legal tourism enterprise, legal, basically does not cover the enterprises prohibited by the law of the land. Thus, 'tourism enterprises' refers to various forms of tourism related activities permissible by the Constitution of India. Like other enterprises, an enterprise in tourism has been based upon some general principles as well as principles specifically associated with tourism entrepreneurship.

According to Sinclair and Stabler (1997), tourism enterprise is a composition of products, such as, transport, accommodation, catering, natural resources, entertainment and other facilities and services including shops, banks and other tour operators. The exhaustive case study placed in this chapter later gives an indepth understsnnding alongwith a detailed picture of tourism scenario in Coastal Odisha while depicting tourism related vocations found in the industry.

Rural entrepreneurship in Tourism— A Case Study

Fields like entrepreneurship in tourism provides broad as well as ever expanding scope for taking the socio-economic status of a region to a new height. The case study that follows proves to be an apt case of tourism entrepreneurship in Odisha.

In rural areas, land, both private and public, is the main source of livelihood in rural areas, with agriculture, animal husbandry, forestry and allied activities. India is emerging as one of the fastest growing economies witnessing a steady GDP growth of around 9 per cent. India is found to leapfrog from an agrarian econmy to a service economy. However, the pace of growth is not homogenous throughout the country. Rural India is unable to match the speed of development and growth of urban India. In India, majority of population live in rural areas, i.e., about 70 per cent. Rural entrepreneurship is viewed as the basis of rural development when it appears to be the essential link in the overall socio-economic development of a region. Further, entrepreneurship is a process where a person is self-employed and is called as an entrepreneur. Hence, entrepreneurship is characterized by self- employment that contributes towards the national income and a balanced economic growth.

Limited availability of land as well as its unequal distribution among the rural people poses a serious problem for full time employment opportunities. Hence, most of the rural farmers and   entrepreneurs in peasant community live Below the Poverty Line (BPL). Besides, rural industrialization has not taken off very far despite adequate attention by the governments and planners alike. India more particularly rural India today increasingly face challenges like employability in addition to unemployment.   When creating additional employment opportunities in rural areas need be focused, entrepreneurship in tourism vocations in rural areas may be considered as a viable solution to such problems.

The economy of Odisha is a balanced mix of agricultural and industrial sectors. Ever since India's independence, the standard of living in Odisha has been below the national average. In contrast to its real per capita income of about 90 per cent of the national average in 1950–51, it came down to about 61 per cent in 2002–03. This declining trend has not only been arrested since 2004–05, but also has reversed. It is found that the gap between the average national per capita income and that of Odisha has been reducing steadily since the year 2004–05. It is again observed that the growth rate of the State has exceeded the national growth rate in five out of last nine years. However, the gap has narrowed down in the last year. Hence, it is the need of the hour to put in extra effort for the State's economy in order to catch up fast with the rest of India.

In this article, an attempt is made to study management of rural entrepreneurship in Odisha tourism with special reference to the socio-economic status of various vocational entrepreneurs in three districts, namely, Puri, Cuttack and Khurda.

Vocations and Tourist Places

Tourism vocations in Odisha may be put in different categories at tourist places in three coastal districts under the study based on the nature of jobs and services rendered by tourism entrepreneurs. Tourism vocations are found in different forms as per the tourist's need and demand. Whether tourist centres are rural or urban, most of the entrepreneurs are the permanent residents of nearby villages. While the villagers lack substantial land and property and source of finance they accept tourism vocation as employment opportunities. In this context, the following table (Table 7.1) presents various vocations available in different tourist places in the coastal districts in question. The table reflects twenty types of tourism entrepreneurs earning their day-to-day livelihood through the occupations mentioned later. The handicraft entrepreneurs may further be categorized into stone work, wood work, patta paintings, horn works, filigree and appliqué work. All these vocations are professionally practised at various tourist places as given in the table.

Table 7.1 Vocations and Tourist Places

Sl.No	Vocations	Tourist Places
1	Priest	Jagannath Temple, Mangala Temple, Alarnath, Barunei, Gouri Temple, Lokanath temple,Gundicha Mandir, Ramachandi, Sun Temple, Sakhigopal, Lingaraj Temple, Dhableswar, Charchika, Bhatarika, Bhagabati, Narayani

Contd.,

Sl.No	Vocations	Tourist Places
2	Bhog, Dhup, Prasad and flower	-do-
3	Shoe stand	-do-
4	Tourist Guide	Puri, Konark, Lingaraj Temple
5	Handicraft	Puri, Cuttack, Konark
6	Stone works	Puri, Konark
7	Wood work	Puri, Konark, Bhubaneswar, Raghurajpur
8	Patta painting	Raghurajpur, Puri
9	Home works	Konark, Puri, Cuttack
10	Filigree	Cuttack
11	Appliqué work	Pipli
12	Photography	Puri, Konark, Bhubaneswar, Satapada, Chilika
13	Swimming facilitator,	Puri, Chandrabhaga
14	Boatman	Chilika, Satapada, Dhabaleswar
15	Restaurants	Puri, Konark, Bhubaneswar, Cuttack, Banpur, Kakatapur, Sakhigopal, Pipli, Balugaon
16	Stationery shop	All places except Ramachandi, Narayani and Raghurajpur
17	Juice-vendor/ Tea stall	All places
18	PCO	All places excluding Narayani & Dhabaleswar
19	Betel shop	All places
20	Horse & camel rider	Puri sea beach

Relatively smaller vocations include photography, swimming facilitator, boatman, etc. Photography is mainly observed in Konark, Puri, Satapada and Chilika, whereas swimming facilitators are specifically seen at sea beaches of Puri and Chandrabhaga. Boatman is a major vocation at Satapada and Chilika lake lagoon as most of the tourists avail boating services. There are shops like stationeries, restaurants, PCOs, betel shops, juice-vendors and mobile vendors who also operate at various tourist centres. In addition to the vocations cited above, horse and camel riding have been found to be popularly attractive only on the beach at Puri. However, for the purpose of analysis, tourist centres have been identified in the three districts on the basis of their historical, religious and cultural importance. It is observed that more tourist spots are located in the districts of Khurda and Puri as well. More tourist spots in Cuttack and Puri districts are outside the towns whereas few spots are found outside the city in Khurda district.

Age Group of the Respondents

All the vocational occupants are classified into four age groups. Age group is an important determinant for one's choice for a vocation. While persons in the higher age group are not likely to quit their vocation, younger persons are likely to switch over to other vocations or professions. While "age" has significant bearing on such decision and the age groups fall between 15–25, 25–35, 35–45 and 45 and above, Table 7.2 depicts these groups. While examining age group of the respondents in various categories, it is observed that most people come in the group of 25–35. It constitutes nearly a third of total occupants taken in the sample. It is followed by the age group of 45 and above with 23.8 per cent.

Priests comprise the major group, i.e., 25 per cent of all the vocational occupants. Majority in this group fall in the age group of 25–35, followed by the age group of 45 and above.

Priests mostly hail from the villages and it is their family tradition to serve in the temples. Those members of the traditional Sevayat families do not find employment elsewhere. After the age of 25, they find little scope for other opportunities and accept priesthood as their permanent occupation. It is seen that the children of these priests who also assist their parents in this vocation fall in the age group of 15–25 while seeking opportunities elsewhere. This can be attributed to the lowest percentage, i.e., 7.7 per cent of the total number of the priests. Further, most among the puja material vendors fall in the age group of 35–45 followed by that of the age between 25 and 35. However, the age group of 15–25 is found to have a significant presence in contrast to rest of the occupations. It implies that there is no marked difference in the number of the respondents falling in different age groups. As a practice, this is also considered as a family tradition, where occupants prefer their children to be engaged in the same.

The pattern of the age groups in case of shoe stand owners demonstrates a different picture. While the age group of 15–25 seems to be dominant, it constitutes as high as 40 per cent of the total sample. The percentage difference between other age groups is found to be small. This indicates that relatively young persons are engaged in this vocation. However, the discussion with these occupants revealed that many of them stay in vocation initially and later switch over to other vocations at the tourist centres or elsewhere. Moreover, photography as a vocation has attracted persons from all the age groups whereas that of 35–45 age bracket seems dominating with 32 per cent.

Table 7.2 Respondents' Age Groups

Sl. No.	Vocations	Years								Total No	
		15 – 25		25 – 35		35 – 45		45 &above			
		1	%	2	%	3	%	4	%	5	%
1	Priest	12	7.7	61	39.1	34	21.8	49	31.4	156	100
2	Pooja material vendors	14	25.4	18	32.7	16	29.0	07	12.9	55	100
3	Shoe stand	06	40.0	03	20.0	04	26.7	02	13.3	15	100
4	Photography	05	20.0	06	24.0	08	32.0	06	24.0	25	100
5	Guide	01	5.0	10	50	04	20.0	05	25.0	20	100
6	Drinks	15	33.3	16	35.6	09	20.0	05	11.1	45	100
7	Nolia	01	6.67	05	33.33	07	46.7	02	13.3	15	100
8	Boatman	03	14.3	10	47.6	06	28.6	02	9.52	21	100
9	Restaurant	14	31.8	14	31.8	05	11.4	11	25.0	44	100
10	Stationery shop	20	38.46	61	39.1	34	21.8	49	31.4	156	100

(Contd.,)

Table 7.2 (Continued)

Sl. No.	Vocations	Years									Total No	
		15 – 25		25 – 35		35 – 45		45 &above				
		1	%	2	%	3	%	4	%	5	%	
11	Peddlers	12	28.6	10	23.8	07	16.7	13	30.9	42	100	
12	Betel shop	11	25.6	09	20.45	09	20.45	15	34.1	44	100	
13	Handicraft	07	11.3	25	40.3	12	19.3	18	29.03	62	100	
14	PCOs	06	27.3	08	36.3	06	27.3	02	9.1	22	100	
15	Entertainment with horse, etc	01	8.33	04	33.33	05	41.7	02	16.7	12	100	
	Total	**128**	**20.3**	**21**	**33.6**	**14**	**22.8**	**14.8**	**23.3**	**630**	**100**	

Source: Primary data collected.

The two other age groups, which include 25–35 and 45 and above employ the same percentage of photographers that is about a fourth. This clearly demonstrates that photographers at the tourist places are evenly distributed so far as the group of age is concerned. The analysis of the age group in respect of the guides indicates that 50 per cent among them fall in the age group of 25–35. As a matter of fact, they need basic education about the places of tourist importance. In order to perform their duty as guides, they also need to communicate in 2–3 languages. This is perhaps the major reason for which they mostly fall in the group of 25–35. Similarly guides are not found in the age group of 15–25 mainly due to the fact that they lack the employable skill for the vocation at that age. Guides are also found seldom in other age groups.

Drink vendors which include green coconut and juice vendors are seen mostly in the age group of 15–25 and 25–35. Relatively senior persons are not engaged in this vocation. However, while the age group of Nolias fuctioning on the beach is analysed, a majority of them fall in the age group 25–35 and 35–45. They need swimming skill as this vocation requires sound health and physique. This is the rationale behind dominance of middle-aged persons in this category. Among the restaurant owners near tourist places, the popular age group appears to be 45 and above, followed by 15–35. It seems that they belong to all age groups while nothing clear emerges from their age analysis. With regard to the stationery shop owners, the predominant age group is 15–25, followed by that of 35–45. The distribution of these occupants in other two groups is almost equal. Moreover, similar trend is observed when we examine the distribution of age group of peddlers and betel shop owners. No specific age group is found to have noticeable presence in this category of the respondents.

However, among the occupants dealing in handicrafts, the majority falls in the age group of 25–35. This is considered reasonable due to the skill necessary for the vocation. While no specific age group is found significant among the PCO owners, the age group of 25–35 is found to dominate among the entertainers. These persons, however,use camels and horses for entertaining the visitors at the tourist places. Children also find this entertainment most attractive and tourist families prefer middle-aged persons to perform these entertainments due to safety of their children. On the overall analysis, it can be inferred that the occupations that demand specific skill and knowledge mostly employ middle-aged persons. In case of other vocations, age distribution of various occupants is almost even exceptionally rare.

Earning Members and Their Dependants

The vocational occupants are mostly local people coming from the countryside. In city areas also majority of them come from the outskirts/bastis. It is observed that most of them practice the vocation on a hereditary basis. Table 7.3 exihibits the earning members working in various occupations and their dependants. In discussion with various vocational occupants, they reply that the number of earning members of the family is either one or two. Generally, majority of them (65 per cent) have one earning member per family whereas, the rest have two.

This trend is found across all the categories of vocations. Nearly 3/4th among the largest group, i.e., priests and puja material vendors replied to have one earning member in their family. However, they seem to express biased opinion. Further, in other vocations, the distribution of respondents shows 65 per cent in one earning member bracket while little higher than a third in two earning member category. This distribution is similar as a general pattern.

Table 7.3 Earning Members and Their Dependants

Vocation	Earning Members				Dependants			
	One		Two		1-3		3-5	
	No	%	No	%	No	%	No	%
Priest	120	76.9	36	23.1	96	61.5	60	39.5
Poojamaterial vendors	45	81.8	10	19.2	32	58.18	23	41.82
Shoe stand	9	60	6	40	10	66.66	5	33.34
Photography	16	64	9	36	15	60	10	40
Guide	12	60	8	40	12	60	8	60
Drinks	32	58.18	13	41.82	26	57.7	19	42.3
Nolia	9	60	6	40	7	46.6	8	63.4
Boatman	14	66.6	7	33.4	11	52.4	10	47.6
Restaurant	25	56.8	19	43.2	30	68.2	14	31.8
Stationery shop	32	61.5	20	38.5	25	38	27	52

Table 7.3　(Continued)

Vocation	Earning Members						Dependants					
	One		Two				1-3		3-5			
	No	%	No	%		No	%		No	%		
Betel shop	30	71.4	12	28.6		25	59.5		17	40.5		
Handicraft	42	62.7	20	32.3		32	51.6		30	48.4		
PCOs	15	68.2	7	31.8		12	54.5		10	45.5		
Entertainers	8	66.6	4	33.4		5	41.6		7	58.4		
Total	**409**	**64.9**	**221**	**35.1**		**338**	**53.7**		**292**	**46.33**		

Source: Primary data collected

The respondents were also asked to state the number of dependents in the family. On the basis of their response, the number of dependents was classified into two groups, i.e., 1–3 and 3–5. The average number of respondents in the first category is 53.7 and the rest is found to be 46.3 in the second category. While all respondents classified vocation-wise, we observe a significant trend. In the larger groups, e.g., priests, puja material vendors and shoe stand owners, the number of dependents is mostly 1–3 with 65 per cent of the respondents found to remain in these categories. In other categories, however, respondents were evenly distributed with regard to the number of dependents. At the same time, the trend seems to be reasonable along the expected lines considering the rural and village base of the respondents.

Qualification

Qualifications possessed by various occupants are displayed in the Table 7.4. Though qualification differs wide across vocations and also in each vocation, a majority of the priests, i.e., 74 per cent are found to be graduates and above,whereas a little over than a tenth and only a tenth among the restaurant owners and guides respectively appear in the class of the under-matriculates. About 64 per cent among the restaurant owners seem to be graduates or above while only 14 per cent of them belong to the category of under-matriculates. This may be attributed to the fact that tiny or small entrepreneurs running restaurants are seen as the least qualified. 39 per cent among the priests happen to be undergraduates whereas 13 per cent belong to the under-matric category. Moreover, as high as 70 per cent among Pooja Samagri vendors are qualified from under graduation to graduation level and above whereas 30 per cent fall under matriculate category. While a fifth of the shoe stand owners are graduates and above, interestingly, the number of shoe stand owners are found to be graduates and above. However, an equal number of shoe stand owners are found to be under-matriculates and undergraduates.

Though as high as 56 per cent among the photographers possess a graduation degree and above, the same for undergraduates and under-matriculates stand at 28 and 6 per cent respectively. Nearly 27 and 18 per cent among the cool drink vendors are undergraduates and above whereas a high percentage of 56 happens to be under-matriculates. Similarly a third among the Nolias are found to be under-matriculates. Whereas, 47 and 20 per cent among them are undergraduates and graduates and above respectively. However, equal number of boatmen seems to be under-matriculates and undergraduates while 23 per cent among them are graduates and above. Furthermore, stationary shop owners are mostly graduates and above while little more than a fifth of them fall in the under-matriculate and undergraduate category alike. Almost a fifth among the peddlers are found to be under and above matriculates while 29 and 52 per cent among them are seen as the under-matriculates and undergraduates respectively. Hardly a fifth among the betel shop owners are found to have graduation or higher qualification while a fifth and significantly 59 per cent of them are seen to be under-matriculates and undergraduates respectively. Besides, 60 per cent among the people handling handicraft business are observed to be undergraduates. Only 15 per cent prove to be under-matriculates. Noticeably, 42 per cent of the entertainers are under-matriculates while a fourth and a third seem to be undergraduates and above.

Table 7.4 Respondents' qualifications

Sl. No	Vocation	Under matric		Under Graduates		Graduates above		Total	
		No	%	No	%	No	%	No	%
1	Priest	21	13.46	61	39.10	74	47.44	156	100
2	Pooja material	16	29.4	25	45.45	14	25.46	55	100
3	Shoe stand	06	40.0	06	40.0	03	20.0	15	100
4	Photography	04	16.0	07	28.0	14	56	25	100
5	Guide	02	10.0	06	30	12	60	20	100
6	Drinks	25	55.55	12	26.67	08	17.78	45	100
7	Nolia	05	33.33	07	46.67	03	20	15	100
8	Boating	08	38.09	08	38.09	05	23.82	21	100
9	Restaurant	06	13.63	10	23.07	28	63.67	44	100
10	Stationery shop	11	21.15	12	52.38	29	55.78	52	100
11	Peddlers	12	28.57	22	20.45	08	19.05	42	100
12	Betel shop	26	59.09	09	59.68	09	20.43	44	100

Table 7.4 (Continued)

Sl. No	Vocation	Under matric		Under Graduates		Graduates above		Total	
		No	%	No	%	No	%	No	%
13	Handicraft	09	14.51	37	36.36	16	25.81	62	100
14	PCOs	02	09.09	08	36.4	12	54.55	22	100
15	Entertainment	05	41.66	03	25.0	04	33.34	12	100
16	Total	141	22.38	250	39.68	239	37.94	630	100

Source: Primary data collected

Monthly Income

Monthly income, an important measure of the occupants'
economic health consists of three groups which are reflected
in Table 7.5. It is noteworthy to record that 76 per cent among
the peddlers earn between ₹4,000 to ₹6,000 per month.
While only a tenth among them and the boatmen earn above
₹6,000 and between two to four thousand rupees respectively.
However as high as 72 per cent of the boatmen earn above
₹6,000. The monthly income of half of the guides goes beyond
₹6,000, whereas a fifth among the guides and drink vendors
earn between 2 to 4 thousand rupees per month. However, an
encouraging figure of about 40 per cent among the priests and
puja material vendors earn beyond ₹6,000 due to favourable
and tourist attracting position of their vocation. Besides, 40
and 27 per cent among the shoe stand owners earn between 4
to 6 thousand rupees and above 6 thousand rupees respectively.
The income of half of the photographers stands between
₹4,000 and ₹6,000 while almost a fourth each earn between
₹2,000 to ₹4,000 and ₹6,000 and more. Furthermore, 40 per
cent of Nolias, the most poverty-stricken among the 15 groups
of vocational occupants, earn between ₹2,000 to ₹4,000 and
about 27 per cent among the restaurant owners earn between
₹2,000 to ₹4,000 whereas a majority of them receive more
than ₹6,000. Also, nearly half of the handicraft and stationary
vendors earn an income of about ₹6,000 per month.

Table 7.5 Monthly Income

Sl.No	Vocational Occupant	2000–4000	%	4000–6000	%	6000 and above	%	Total No	%
1	Priest	35	22.4	60	38.5	61	39.1	156	100
2	Pooja material	10	29.4	11	32.4	34	38.2	55	100
3	Shoe stand	05	33.3	06	40	04	26.7	15	100
4	Photography	06	24	13	50	07	25	26	100
5	Guide	04	20	06	30	10	50	20	100
6	Drinks	09	20	24	53.3	12	26.7	45	100
7	Nolia	06	40	07	46.7	02	13.3	15	100
8	Boatman	02	9.5	04	19	15	71.5	21	100
9	Restaurant	12	27.3	09	20.5	23	52.2	44	100
10	Stationery shop	09	17.3	24	46.2	19	36.5	52	100
11	Peddlers	06	14.3	32	76.2	04	9.5	42	100
12	Betel shop	12	27.3	20	45.5	12	27.2	44	100
13	Handicraft	07	11.3	25	40.3	30	48.4	62	100

Sl.No	Vocational Occupant	2000-4000	%	4000-6000	%	6000 and above	%	Total No	%
14	PCOs	07	31.8	08	36.4	07	31.8	22	100
15	Entertainment	02	16.7	06	50	04	33.3	12	100
16	Total	132	40.3	254	38.7	249	38.7	630	100

Source: Primary data collected

Encouragement to Children to Adopt the Vocation

Table 7.6 shows the number and percentage of vocational occupants interested to see their children to continue their existing occupation. Most significant among them, i.e., three-fourth of the entertainers reject the vocation to be occupied by their own children. However, 52 per cent among the handicraft stall owners refuse their children to adopt the vocation. Nearly 28 per cent among the priests are interested for acceptance of the occupation by their children while about 73 per cent refuse. Among the puja material vendors little more than a third reply in affirmative whereas twice of that reply negatively. Similarly, as high as 73 per cent say no for inheriting the vocation by their children while the remaining show their preference for the same. Further, 40 per cent each among the guides, drink vendors and Nolias give a positive reply and the rest say no. Photographers (44 per cent) give a positive reply whereas 56 per cent answer in negative. Even 57 per cent among the boatmen and 68 per cent restaurant owners with comparatively higher investment in their vocation give a negative reply. Likewise, the respective percentage in case of stationery shop and handicraft stall owners with a sizable investment and positive opinion stand at 27 per cent and 48 per cent.

In case of the peddlers and betel shop owners, 71 to 73 per cent give a negative reply for inheritance by their children whereas 68 per cent among the PCO proprietors also disapprove and reject such hereditary business. Mostly, it is found that one-third across all the occupants give their assent for their children to accept the vocation and two-third reject the same.

Table 7.6 Encouragement to Children Adopting the Vocation

Sl.No	Vocational occupants	Yes		No		Total	
		No	%	No	%	No	%
1	Priest	43	27.56	113	72.54	156	100
2	Pooja materials	19	34.54	36	65.46	55	100
3	Shoe stand	4	26.67	11	73.34	25	100
4	Photography	11	44	14	56	15	100
5	Guide	8	40	12	60	20	100
6	Drinks	18	40	27	60	45	100
7	Nolia	6	40	09	60	15	100
8	Boatman	9	42.9	12	57.1	21	100
9	Restaurant	14	31.8	30	68.2	44	100
10	Stationery shop	14	26.9	38	73.1	52	100
11	Peddlers	12	28.6	30	71.4	42	100
12	Betel shop	12	27.27	32	72.73	44	100

Table 7.6 (Continued)

Sl.No	Vocational occupants	Yes		No		Total	
		No	%	No	%	No	%
13	Handicraft	30	48.4	32	51.6	62	100
14	PCOs	07	31.8	15	68.2	22	100
15	Entertainment	03	25.0	09	75.0	12	100
16	Total	210	33.33	420	66.67	630	100

Source: Primary data collected

Level of Satisfaction

The respondents were asked to point out their satisfaction level in their own vocations. The summary of their opinions as presented in Table 7.7 reveals that none of the respondents are found highly satisfied. Equally significant to note is that none of the respondents expressed moderate satisfaction from their respective vocations. The mean score is below 3.0 for all vocations excepting two vocations that is photography and restaurants. The average score is just above 3, i.e., 3.1 in both the cases. Some vocations, i.e., shoe stand, guides, nolia and boatmen express almost dissatisfaction with their occupations as the mean score for these vocations is less than 0.015.

Table 7.7   Level Of Satisfaction

Sl.No	Vocational occupants	Mean	Standard deviation
1	Priest	2.5	.014
2	Pooja materials	2.6	.021
3	Shoe stand	1.8	.013
4	Photography	3.1	.012
5	Guide	1.8	.013
6	Drinks	2.4	.012
7	Nolia	1.9	.014
8	Boatmen	1.8	.013
9	Restaurant	3.1	0.14
10	Stationary shop	2.9	.020
11	Peddlers	2.2	.011
12	Betel shop	2.6	.014
13	Handicraft	2.8	.015
14	PCOs	1.8	.015
15	Entertainment	1.2	.020
	Total	**2.35**	**22.38**

At the lower end of the satisfaction, we also find the vocation like, priests, puja material vendors, drinks, handicrafts, stationary shops, etc.

Furthermore, we observe that the respondent's opinions are not totally free from bias. They present varying opinions, often contradictory in nature. However, the trend of satisfaction level is clear and creates a scope for devising means of strengthening their vocations with a view to raise/improve satisfaction. The overall average score of satisfaction level is 2.35 which signifies less than moderate satisfaction. This kind of opinion was also expected from them as many expressed pessimism over continuing or improving the vocation.

Factors Responsible for Decline of the Vocation

Finally, the views of various respondents were sought regarding the factors chiefly responsible for the decline in vocations. Interestingly majority of the respondents attributed insufficient earning as the most significant factor. While they attributed their dissatisfaction to the lack of communication and amenities available at the tourist centres, the next important factor was highlighted as to the polluted environment. Absence of proper sanitation and security were considered detrimental to the tourism vocations at various tourist places. The next significant factor in order of the weightage happened to be non-cooperation of the government agencies for the development of tourism and related vocations.

The above response of the tourism entrepreneurs are corroborated by the degree of satisfaction level in their respective vocations as presented in Table-7.7. However, the respondents were not prepared to accept some of the other factors such as high cost of vocation, fall in tourist inflows and disinterest of the tourists which may be responsible for the decline of the vocation.

CONCLUSION

Seemingly Odisha is prosperous in terms of huge mineral deposits underneath its soil while facing abject poverty on top of its soil. Its economy is a balanced mix of agricultural and industrial sector. The state is also home to many beautiful tourist destinations. Besides, Odisha, the house to 3.57 per cent of Indian population is both Mao-infested and a victim of nature's vagaries. More than 80 per cent of its inhabitants live in rural areas mostly depending on agriculture. At the same time growing unemployment, particularly the educated unemployed youth, poses one of the baffling problems for the state. Trapped between the problem of unemployment on the one hand and lack of quality employees on the other , the Government of Odisha is seriously concerned for being unable to optimally exploit the benefits out of its ongoing mega-industrialization drive.

Against this backdrop, rich natural and human resources in Odisha offer a huge potential for tourism development and its related vocations. Tourism is looked upon to provide a vast innovative scope for development of several vocations. Large-scale unemployment and ever increasing poverty in the state underscore the need for tapping tourism resource and exploring new avenues of tourism. Moreover, tourism in coastal Odisha has emerged as an activity resulting in a number of socio-economic benefits. The nature of employment, skilled and unskilled, seasonal and perennial provided by tourism is found to be significant. Majority among vocational occupiers at the tourist places under the study are either unskilled or semi-skilled. However, tourism also provides indirect employment to many rural people outside the industry, i.e., those who provide goods and services to those directly engaged in the industry.

Odisha occupies a prominent position in the tourist map of India. There is a bright future for tourism and hospitality industry here. Endowed with some of India's best kept culture secrets from the outside world, it offers a multidimensional experience spanning rich architectural monuments, a golden coastline, wildlife, art and craft. As a result, Odisha tourism not only attracts domestic tourists but also international tourists. The state having all the favourable tourist potentials, due attention should be given by the planners, policy makers as well as by the Governments of State and the Centre for tourism development in order to attain a higher rate of economic growth by reducing the BPL population and empowering rural Odisha.

REFERENCES

1. Aghion, P.N., Bloom, R., Blundell, R. Griffith and P.Howitt. (2005) "Competition and innovation an Inverted u-relationship Quarterly Journal of Economics 120(2).

2. Alesina, A. and D. Rodrik. (1994). "Distributive Policies and Economic Growth". *Quarterly Journal of Economics.* 109.

3. Barro, R. (2000). "Inequality and Growth in a Panel of Countries". *Journal of Economic Growth.* vol. 5.

4. Commission on Growth & Development. (2008). Growth Report: Strategies for Sustained Growth and Inclusive Development, The World Bank.

5. Khanka, S.S. (2011): Developing Tourism Entrepreneurship in India: Perspectives and Prospects, innnnnn Y. Venkata Rao

and G. Anjaneya Swamy (Eds.) Tourism Entrepreneurship, Excel Books, New Delhi.

6. Sida. (2006). Integrated Economic Analysis for Pro-poor Growth: A Methodological Approach, Method Document. Stockholm: Sida

7. Sinclaire, M.T., and M. Stabler (1997): The Economics of Tourism, Routledge, London.

8. Sussex: Institute of Development Studies OECD (2008). Growing Unequal Income Distribution and Poverty in OECD Countries.

9. The Economic Survey, Government of Odisha, Various Issues..

10. World Bank Economic Review, vol. 10, pp. 565–91.

8

MICRO AND SMALL ENTREPRISES

INTRODUCTION

Micro enterprises defy a definition. Street vendors, carpenters, machine shop operators, seamstresses and peasant farmers—micro entrepreneurs come in all types, and their businesses in many sizes. This diverse group requires a variety of support to grow and improve. While many of these men and women and their employees are poor, they do not lack the potential despite their limited access to services. With their number growing up to some 50 million, they can hardly be considered marginal. Being viewed as the heart of a region's economy, they account for as much as half of all employment in many countries. They contribute significantly to economic growth, social stability and equity. However, more than 80 per cent of the businesses in Latin America and the Caribbean have 10 employees or less. In fact, this sector proves to be one of the most important vehicles through which low-income people can escape poverty. With limited skills and education to compete for formal sector jobs, these men and women find economic opportunities in micro enterprise as business owners and employees. For example, in Chile, a Banco del Desarrollo evaluation points out that 88 per cent of the bank's micro enterprise clients representing the poorest groups, have dramatically improved their standard of living after receiving a loan.

Small firms contribute considerably to economic growth. They employ a very large number of people, second only to agriculture. One of the learning shared by seasoned and successful entrepreneurs is that start ups cannot afford to pass on any opportunity, no matter how small. One needs to see business much like a game of Pac Man, you can beg big fish only by learning to swallow small ones. The biggest advantage of starting small is that it allows you to find out what the industry and market is all about and make mistakes when one can still afford it. Growth, when it comes, is all the more sustainable as a result. Although many aspects of entrepreneurship favor the young, patience does not. Here experience has an edge. Impatience often pushes new entrepreneurs to blindly adopt a get big fast philosophy or going for scale. This approach only makes sense in certain contexts, especially for businesses like on-line recruitment sites, as their competitive advantage lies in the size of their networks. But it does not work for most start ups.

Take the case of Infosys. It took over 13 years before it started experiencing growth. Prior to that, people had not even heard of the company. Reliance started small selling door-to-door before it moved to other areas and grew big. Every major success story in corporate India today speaks of the same lesson. Start small, learn the ropes, dig in your feet and then expand at the right time and opportunity. Infosys's growth coincided with the need for US companies to offshore their development, that of Reliance with the opening market which needed players of scale, etc. While they mostly concentrate in the urban areas, rural areas have, by and large, failed to seize the opportunities unleashed by India's economic reforms. Besides, little is known about the characteristics of rural entrepreneurs who take up entrepreneurship because they do not find better opportunity and only incidentally due to their interest. Government as well as private agencies have attempted at different models of rural entrepreneurship in order to tap the potential of human resource as an engine of growth. Here, it would be most appropriate to quote Aavishkaar, a Fund dedicated to the development of Rural Entrepreneurship which says, "We firmly believe we can leverage rural innovations and appropriate technologies to create viable and sustainable micro ventures. This will spur economic activity, create productive jobs and improve quality of life.

ESSENTIAL CHARACTERISTICS

The characteristics of the MSEs can be explained under the following points:

i.   An MSE can be very well a one-man show.

ii. The owner in case of micro enterprises works as its manager. She/he actively participates in decision-making. With one's firsthand knowledge of the business, such entrepreneur runs the enterprise in one's personal style of functioning.

iii. A micro industrial unit has comparatively a shorter gestation period.

iv. Indigenous resources are usually used in micro enterprise. Thus, these units are located in areas having availability of resource like labour and raw material.

v.   MSEs are found dispersed across country's rural areas, as they are very much in need of local resources. This phenomenon checks rural exodus while resulting in balanced regional development.

vi.   MSEs not only need limited capital investment but also prove to be fairly labour-intensive.

vii.   Small-scale units are highly adaptive in terms of introduction of new product, new material, market and form of organization.

RATIONALE BEHIND MSEs

In order to understand the rationale behind MSEs, The Industrial Policy Resolution, 1956 can be aptly cited here. It states, "Small-scale enterprises provide immediate large-scale employment, they offer a method of ensuring a more equitable distribution of the national income and they facilitate an effective mobilization of resources of capital and skill which might otherwise remain unutilized. Some of the problems that unplanned urbanization tends to create will be avoided by the establishment of small centres of industrial production all over the country". In view of the above readings of the 1956 IPR, the rationale behind origin and growth of the MSEs can be highlighted below in greater detail.

i.   **Employment Generation**   This argument of employment creation through MSEs seems more justified in developing countries like India for abundance of labour and scarcity of resource. In the light of several research findings, MSEs are more labour intensive for which they prove to be more relevant in the developing world characterized by massive unemployment. Such argument has, however, been vehemently opposed by scholars like Dhar and Lydall(1961), who opine that employment should not be created for the sake of employment. Also, it is not crucial to absorb the resource that is surplus, but to optimally use the scarce resource. According to them, the argument of employment becomes an output argument.

ii. **Equality** The ownership in case of the MSEs is more broad-based and dispersed. Besides, their labour-intensiveness and decentralization among the rural and less backward areas result in more equitable distribution of their produce. They promote greater employment to the unemployed ensuring more equitable distribution of national income and wealth.

iii. **Latent Resource** MSEs can tap unutilized and latent resource including idle manpower and hoarded wealth. According to Dhar and Lyndall, there is no dearth of entrepreneurial skill in India, wheras resource lie idle. Hence, they reject the ability of MSEs to efficiently mop up a region's existing idle resource. However, post-Independence growth of entrepreneurship brings home this fact that provision of financial and physical infrastructure can adequately promote MSEs so as to enable them to tap the latent resource.

iv. **Decentralization** In contrast to the MSEs, big enterprises are more likely to concentrate in urban areas. Though, it is not possible to set up MSE in every village, it is quite viable to start them in a cluster approach (group of villages). Such dispersal of MSE units can mop up available resources like idle savings, local talent and raw material, etc., leading to the much talked about inclusive growth.

SCOPE OF MSEs IN INDIA

The government of India has announced its policy of reservation for small sector chiefly comprising of micro enterprise units. The main objective of the reservation policy is to insulate the MSE sector from unequal competition from large business establishments. The industries reserved for exclusive development in the MSE include: textile, food and allied industries; Leather; rubber products; plastic products, Natural essential oils, Organic Chemicals and Chemical products; Glass and Ceramic, Bicycle parts; Stationery items, etc. As many as 47 items were reserved by The reservation Policy initiated in1967 for exclusive manufacture by the small-scale sector. By 1983, the list of reservation included 836 items for such exclusive production. However, the Abid Hussain Committee has later dereserved 12 items, leaving 824 items under the reserved category. Unfortunately, the performance of non-reserved MSEs outweighs those of the reserved micro and small enterprises. According to some research, poor performance of such Government funded MSEs under reserve category can be attributed to 'easy' entry into the MSE sector resulting in excess supply and therby, a reduction in their profitability.

WOMEN IN MICRO ENTERPRISES

Women-owned businesses make up one of the fastest growing segments of micro enterprise. As micro entrepreneurs, women not only contribute significantly to national income, they also create reliable social safety nets for their families and communities. The work women do outside the home is usually in addition to the care they provide for their families, which limits their business opportunities. Moreover, they often face even greater obstacles than their male counterpart in getting credit from formal sources. Increased income in the hands of women is invested in health, education and housing for their families. In Latin America and the Caribbean, women own and operate 30-60 per cent of such companies.

MSE PERSPECTIVES SINCE 1990s

Post-reform era in India has brought in an entrepreneurial economy (though some of the old aristocrats have been replaced by a few oligarchs). It has swept the country to a new ways of life, unmatched on this gigantic scale anywhere in the world. Fortunately, today's knowledge-based economy has proved to be a fertile ground for entrepreneurs vis-à-vis small entrepreneurs.

One of the most significant global changes witnessed during 1990s is the increasing use of public-private partnership approaches to finance infrastructure development and in other areas with the assumption that the benefits of such partnerships would trickle down in the system leading to the creation of better living conditions. The 1993 UNDP Workshop also emphasized the need to create an institutional mechanism at a micro level which should be flexible, low in cost and simple in procedure for providing finances and rendering support services at close proximity to the borrower. As a result of the efforts for promoting an innovative mechanism for providing finance and support services to MSEs, two corporate entities have been established in India. Indian Micro Enterprises Development Foundation (IMEDF), incorporated in 1996 as a not-for-profit organization, and Indian Micro Enterprises Development Finance Corporation Limited (IMEDFIN) incorporated in 1997 as a for-profit entity. IMEDFIN provides credit to the MSE sector using innovative financial instrumentalities (including venture capital financing). The working of the Foundation and the Corporation together is an initiative towards developing an innovative Indian model in order to cater to that class of people who are otherwise excluded from the formal credit system due to lack of material collateral. The joint effort also provide support service input to promote sustainable enterprises.

Furthermore, in the formal sector, two common sources of failure of development financial intermediaries are imperfect information and imperfect enforcement. The Foundation and the Corporation have plans to strategically tackle this gap by setting up an information centre to have a strong database. For the purpose of the Corporation and the Foundation, MSEs have been defined to include those enterprises which have a total investment in plant and equipment ranging from ₹10,000 to ₹10 lakhs and from ₹10 lakhs to ₹1 crore, respectively and whose operations/outputs are eco-friendly and technology-based with inputs of market-driven indigenous or imported technology. Besides, the Foundation helps create an enabling environment for MSEs while it provides support services to Micro Small Entrepreneurs and Micro Credit Finance Institutions in the NGO Sector.

A Tanzanian Case Study

This article explores the nature of micro credit, in rural Tanzania. It begins by examining the types of finance available to the poor running micro enterprises. The intended role and availability of micro credit in alleviating poverty is considered. Most institutes which offer loan facilities operate mainly in urban centres, thus restricting accessibility for the rural poor. Moreover, the modest lending conditions also create an obstacle for the poorest women. The empirical part of the study examines the impact of one institution, the SELF project which is specifically intended to address these issues. By means of a survey, SELF loans have been found to have some benefits in improving the profitability of micro enterprises run by rural poor women, but there seems to have little long-term effect as measured by increases in household assets.

An Indian Case

Poverty and resultant starvation in India is not limited to the lower caste, although they suffer the most. The lower caste forms only about 20% of the Indian population, whereas starvation and malnourishment affect about 53% of its entire population. Against this backdrop, the case as given here explicates entrepreneurship as a means to empower the underprivileged sections, particularly the scheduled castes. The cases of the scheduled castes from Jalandhar and Amritsar (cities of Punjab) reveal that they have experienced social, economic and political mobility through entrepreneurship. The entrepreneurial activities are, however, unevenly distributed among the rural and urban scheduled castes. It is mainly the two scheduled caste groups, namely, the *Ad-dharmi* and the *Megh*, in both the cities, who have ventured into entrepreneurship, largely by diversifying their traditional caste occupations The *Ad-dharmis* have modified their skills in handling and processing the rawhides and have started leather-based industries, factories and workshops. The *Meghs*, who have been engaged as workers in the manufacturing of surgical instruments before migrating to these cities from Sialkot after the partition of India (1947), have excelled in sports goods and surgical instruments industries.

As the study reveals, the overall empowerment of scheduled castes is possible through entrepreneurship. The policy makers may encourage entrepreneurship as a means to achieve equality for them. In India, the MSEs have proved to be an engine of growth of the economy with a substantial proportion of India's exports being generated by the segment. Recognizing the importance of this employment-intensive segment, the National Common Minimum Programme (NCMP) of the government has declared to free the sector from Inspector Raj and be given full credit, technology and marketing support. A package of policy measures for strengthening and enhancing support to the MSEs is another significant declaration in the NCMP. Also as a major step, the Government has announced a policy package for stepping up credit to SMEs (including micro/tiny enterprises). This package provide for doubling the flow of credit to these enterprises within five years and ensuring 20-per cent year to year growth. Fulfilling another commitment in the NCMP, the Government has constituted the National Commission of Enterprises in the unorganized sector to examine the problem faced by such enterprises and make appropriate recommendations. The National Manufacturing Competitiveness Council (NMCC) has also been constituted by the Government to recommend measures for enhancing the competitiveness of India's manufacturing industries, SMEs in the main.

PROBLEMS OF MSE

An enterprise has always the need for working capital and investment purposes. While the formal sector venture is well serviced by commercial banks and other financial institutions, informal units suffer from extreme shortage of all types of resources. The shortage of funds makes it difficult to maintain even minimum inventories and tap favourable market opportunities. Official policies often make business difficult for the MSEs. Though an improved business regulations, tax regimes, financial sector reform and bank supervision promote better conditions for microenterprise development, less than five percent of Latin American micro-entrepreneurs have access to formal financial services. Deposit services are rarely geared to these business people, especially in rural areas. Besides, small loan requirements of micro-entrepreneurs usually are less attractive to traditional formal financial institutions because of their high transaction costs. Micro-entrepreneurs also lack access to services such as marketing, training in basic business skills, and technology transfer.

Further, with almost 80 per cent of the Indians fighting for their survival every day, it is of utmost importance to identify new ways and means to provide resources for them for better livelihood. Grant or subsidies are far too small in macro-economic terms to do much in the face of the vastness of the problem. There is also a need to find ways to encourage survivors rather than creating helpless dependents. This, however, necessitates a basic change in the mindset of both givers and takers. One sustainable way of dealing with the situation is to create sustainable livelihoods. Government agencies and the formal sector clearly cannot absorb the entire workforce. In this scenario, there is a need to promote entrepreneurship, particularly the MSEs in the informal sector.

CONCLUSION

Micro and small enterprises encompass vast scope covering activities such as manufacturing, servicing, retailing, construction, financing, infrastructure, etc. In view of the Government of India's ever increasing importance given to the MSEs in the national economy, more and more MSEs need to be promoted in the future days. Presently, India has 45 million entrepreneurs—most building small businesses, some building big businesses—but all contributing to an economy that boasts a middle class as big as the entire population of the United States. Besides, today's knowledge-based economy has been a fertile ground for entrepreneurs vis-à-vis small entrepreneurs. In India, the MSEs have proved to be an engine of growth of the economy with a substantial proportion of the nation's exports. India has come along faster than anyone would have expected, and there are good reasons to believe these trends can continue. Here, the dismantling of the License Raj and ushering of reforms destroyed the old aristocracy and feudalism. Indeed, it brought in an entrepreneurial economy (though some of the old aristocrats have been replaced by a few oligarchs). It has swept the country to new ways of life, unmatched on this gigantic scale anywhere in the world.

Small producers, who traditionally have no access to institutional credit, have greater needs for training and technical assistance as well. Therefore, it is becoming increasingly important for the lending agency to work in association with, or in coordination with, promotional agencies specializing in training and technical assistance for informal activities. At the same time, it is important to find ways to make the financial operations attractive and profitable in funding small scale operations to attract the inflow of funds. To be, however, able to meet the credit needs of a small, informal unit, financial intermediaries have to reduce the relatively high operating costs, increase revenue, and undertake organizational adaptation. It is of utmost importance, therefore, to have an efficient and competent promotion agency with experience or capability of quickly adapting to the circumstances. Besides, it requires a financial intermediary that agrees to adjust requirements, criteria and procedures, without sacrificing financial viability.

ROLE OF MICRO ENTERPRISE IN LIVELIHOOD PROMOTION

A PERSPECTIVE STUDY IN INDIA

1. INTRODUCTION

Micro enterprises are the heart of a region's economy. They contribute significantly to economic growth, social stability and equity. They account for as much as half of all employment in many countries. The micro enterprise sector proves to be one of the most important vehicles which help the low-income people escape poverty. Even, in situations of entrenched poverty, micro enterprises arguably offer women a way of supporting themselves and their families. However, micro enterprise defies a definition. Street vendors, carpenters, machine shop operators and peasant farmers—micro entrepreneurs come in all types, and their businesses in many sizes. This diverse group requires a variety of support to grow and improve. Many of these men and women and their employees are poor with limited access to services. Traditionally, these informal sector units including micro and small enterprises (MSEs) are used to attract a very small portion of the banks' portfolio. Equally important, MSEs need adequate funds from the lenders by making their operations attractive and profitable. In view of this, the formal sector banks, with their dismal performance in loan recovery and the unsustainable level of non-performing assets (NPAs), have revisited their policies on priority sector lending.

Furthermore, in the process of bringing innovations in the lending policies, planners and the policy makers have received valuable inputs from the success of micro credit programmes in Bangladesh, Bolivia, Indonesia, Zambia regarding feasibility of the group-based saving and lending mechanism. The pioneering role played by Grammeen Bank in Bangladesh in reaching the poorest of the poor signifies that the poor are bankable. The tremendous impact of the micro credit program through self-help groups (SHGs) introduced by Grammen Bank have also established the usefulness of village-level institutions in poverty elimination and underdevelopment. Above all, the success of micro credit programs all over the world has received wider acceptance among the development planners to adopt this as an alternative development strategy. In a United Nations Development Programme (UNDP) workshop in Delhi, in collaboration with the World Business Council for Sustainable Development on MSEs and Eco-friendly Technology in the year 1993, World Business Council for Sustainable Development, Canada and Development Alternatives, New Delhi spelt out and demonstrated the MSEs and sustainable development linkages based on experiences of FUNDES[1], and TARA[2]. (Savyasachi Achla, 1998). The workshop recommended steps to create an institutional mechanism in India to provide finances and support services to the MSEs for promoting sustainable livelihoods and providing income-generating opportunities.

Meanwhile, in India, three major developments have taken place in the recent years with significant impact on the rural economy especially the rural poor. They include:

    (i) the economy experienced a robust growth

---

1.   An institution to promote micro enterprises based in Latin America.

2.   The micro enterprises arm of Development Alternatives.

(ii) National Rural Employment Guarantee Scheme (NREGS) emerged as a major programme to provide additional income to the rural poor and

(iii) various initiatives taken under the National Skill Development Mission (NSDM) in order to achieve the objective of the 11th Plan (2007–12) of broad based inclusive growth.

In this perspective, Strategy Paper of the Ministry of the Rural Development has envisaged a four pronged strategy to attack rural poverty comprising:

(i)   generation of self employment in credit linked micro enterprises

(ii) wage employment under the NREGS

(iii) payment of pension to elderly and vulnerable sections under National Social Assistance Programme

(iv) income generation and social security programmes of other Ministries of Government of India.

Taking these policy initiatives into account, the restructuring of Swarn Jayanti Gram Swarojgar Yojana (SGSY) as National Rural Livelihood Mission was conceived as a corner stone of national poverty reduction strategy[3].

---

3. The SGSY Scheme, implemented in all states except *Delhi* and *Chandigarh* since 1999, was primarily designed to promote self-employment oriented income generating activities for the BPL households in the rural areas. Woven around the mechanism of SHGs, the SGSY has been designed to break the financial, technical and market constraints that the individual BPL households face to cross the threshold of poverty line The main components of the scheme include:

(i)   formation of SHGs;

(ii) capacity building training and skill training to take up micro-enterprises;

(iii) strengthening thrift and credit in SHGs;

In this context, microfinance as a means for alleviating poverty has gained momentum in the last couple of decades across India vis-à-vis Odisha, a province fraught with the twin problems of poverty and unemployment. While it assumes significance for a Mao-infested province like Odisha, the units in this informal MSE sector operate under the conditions of extreme resource crunch. Against this backdrop, the present paper has made an attempt to make a comparative study of two microfinance institutions (MFIs) operating in Odisha, i.e., Adhikar and People's Forum (PF) with their headquarters at Bhubaneswar, the Provincial capital city. Besides, it explores the fact whether the borrowers have an understanding and appreciation for the facility of MF being provided to them in an Indian Province, called Odisha.

IMPACT OF SCALING UP OF MF TO THE MSE SECTOR AND AN ANALYSIS OF THE FINANCIAL GAP

An assessment was made to highlight the prospects, challenges and implications of scaling up MF to the MSE sector followed by an analysis of the financial gap, if any. Keeping this in view, the following objectives have been set:

i. To review the working of Adhikar and People's Forum.

ii. To study the financial performance of both the MFIs

iii. To assess the role of the two in empowering the members of the SHG/JLGs (Joint Liability Groups).

iv. To examine their role in women empowerment.

(iv) credit linkage with banks/other financial institutions and back ended subsidy for eligible SHGs/members to take up micro enterprises; and

(vi) technology inputs for micro enterprises.

The present assessment is based on the data collected from the primary as well as secondary sources. Primary data have been collected through meetings coupled with focus group interviews and interactions with various officials of the MFIs in question, inter alia, their beneficiaries selected at random. Methods like questionnaire survey, face-to-face interactions have been used for the purpose, while the assessment has collected opinions of the executives of Adhikar and PF. Besides, secondary data have been collected from their annual reports, leaf lets and brochures, various published magazines and books. However, relevant and valuable information, to some extent, have been available from their respective websites. Certain limitations are, also, observed due to non-availability of adequate published literature material. Moreover, as sustainable livelihood literature and practice are relatively new, some gaps have been realized in the course of this assessment.

Micro and Small Enterprise and Livelihood Promotion

An enterprise, whether in formal or informal sector, needs financial resources for working capital and investment purposes. While the formal sector is well serviced by various commercial banks and other financial institutions, informal units operate under the conditions of extreme shortage of all types of resources. These include a poor endowment of fixed capital and working capital. The low level of working capital forces small producers to buy inputs in small quantity resulting in considerable loss of time and interruption in production processes. However, small loan needs of the MSEs seem to be less attractive to traditional formal financial institutions, while micro entrepreneurs lack access to services such as marketing, training and technology transfer. Besides, formal financial institutions prefer to finance a customer with sufficient assets that can be pledged as security. Secondly, these institutions consider recovery of their portfolio as the only major factor worth considering. They are not determining the composition of the portfolio according to the needs of the financial resources of the informal sector. Thus, both qualitative and quantitative limitations of the MSEs in terms of access to outdated technologies, lead to a low level of productivity and extremely high cost.

Equally important, micro, small and medium enterprises (MSMEs) now contribute 8 per cent of the national GDP (Gross Domestic Product), while the Ministry of MSME implements the credit linked subsidy scheme for assisting these units to acquire upgraded technology. Of late, the Union Government of India has instructed the banks to give 60 per cent of the MSME advances to the micro enterprises in order to augment supply of funds to them. As aptly put by the Union Minister, MSME, "The banks have been told to allocate 50 per cent of MSME advances towards the micro-enterprises in the Financial Year 2010–11, 55 per cent in 2011–12 and 60 per cent by the end of 2013."[4] Again, it is worth mentioning here that most among the nationalised banks and formal credit institutions advance loans to enterprises that have a relatively solid bottom line and sufficient financial data. This is, in fact, available to some of the well-performing small and medium enterprises (SMEs). Hence, the cultural gap between the institutions and the community that needs to be bridged is wide.

---

4. Adapted from His Speech in a Seminar, "Competitiveness Through Finance and Technology" organized by the Indian Chamber of Commerce, The Times of India, Ibid.

Further, the formal financial institutions usually being accustomed to deal with the more confident, literate borrower of urban areas, there is another financial system: **"Microfinance."** Its targets are not only poor and low-income groups, but also micro enterprises. The main objective of MF activity is to alleviate poverty and generation of employment for those poor people who are excluded from formal financial services. Undeniably, the failure of the formal banking sector to ensure financial inclusion of the poor and marginalized section has promoted an ever increasing number of MFIs to carry forward this agenda. The MFIs, indeed, create and strengthen the livelihood opportunities. Basically, they satisfy the credit needs of the people excluded from the economic, social, and political mainstream and unable to participate in SL (Sustainable Livelihood) activities. They also provide opportunities to move ahead by promoting the livelihoods and thus empowering the targeted and disadvantaged.

Indian perspective of microfinance, in the last few years, has witnessed an unprecedented growth and has firmly established itself as a significant and potential financial contributor to the Government and the society at large. While, more than 2.2 million SHGs are credit linked by the banks under the SHG bank linkage programme, an additional 10 million clients are served through the MFI channel. On the lines of the success story scripted by Grameen Bank, Bancosol in Bolivia, Bank Rakyat in Indonesia, SEWA and MYRADA in India have been able to implement the micro-credit programmes successfully[5]. On the top of this, formal financial institutions in the country have been playing a leading role in the MF programme for more than two decades now. They have joined hands proactively with informal delivery channels to

5.   Meher, S., SHGs and Poverty in Orissa (2003).

give MF sector the necessary momentum. Towards the end of the previous decade too, MF has registered an impressive expansion at the grassroot level[6]. According to a banker,[7] the factor that fuelled the stratospheric rise of MFIs was the fortuitous priority sector lending clause issued by the Reserve Bank of India (RBI). Under this clause, banks have to lend 40 per cent of their total loan portfolio, out of which, 45 per cent should go to agriculture. In case of the failure to meet this target, banks were supposed to stash this cash in the bonds issued by National Bank of Agriculture and Rural Development (NABARD), which fetched a paltry 3–4 per cent interest. While the private sector banks found it difficult to meet the target for priority sector lending, MFIs became a God-sent for delivering 12–13 per cent interest. When the RBI insisted that MF could be treated as agriculture loans, both banks and MFIs rejoiced and business with each other started booming.

Against this backdrop, the Millennium Declaration of the UN identifies poverty alleviation as one of the most crucial challenges that the international community is facing in the 21st century. With nearly 40 per cent of the Indians living below the poverty line, top most priority is given to identify new ways and means to provide resources for better livelihoods. According to The UN Annual Millennium Development Goal (MDG) Report, "India has played a crucial role in eradicating poverty from the world"[8]. The fact that India was a "major contributor" to poverty reduction has also been acknowledged in the UN Secretary General's Report

6. Status of Micro Finance in India-2007–08, National Bank for Agriculture & Rural Development, Mumbai.
7. Business Standard, Dated 18th August, 2011.
8. The Dharitri, Odisha, Bhubaneswar, Dated 9th July, 2011.

on MDGs[9]. In the wake of a global economic slowdown, the growth in India's GDP during the last one decade has been commendable. The country also recorded the highest growth rate of billionaires who made it to the Forbes' list. Their number also doubled in one year to reach a figure of 55 in 2011. India's factory sector expanded at its slowest pace in more than two years in August last as export orders shrank amid weakening weak global demand. Still, India has been one of the few countries to show growth[10]. Also, in the words of the economist, Jagdish Bhagwati, India is ready for a "revolution of perceived possibilities", in which reforms can produce high economic returns along with improvements for the poor. Indian democracy to be meaningful, development has to be inclusive, comprehensive and extensive. We have to empower all the Indians by making them partners in growth and beneficiaries of development.

At the same time, on the face of the above said growth rate, the increase in the number of employed people in 2005–2010 has not been commensurate with the high GDP growth rate of 8.6 per cent during the same period.[11] Further, in the words of the Economist and Prime Minister, "Grants or subsidies are far too small in macro-economic terms to do much in the face of the vastness of the problem". Government agencies and the formal sector clearly cannot absorb the entire work force. It, in fact, calls for an increasing need to promote entrepreneurship in the informal sector, particularly, the much talked about MSE sector.

---

9. The Times of India, Dated 14th November, 2010.
10. The findings of A Survey of the Manufactures in Asia's third largest Economy, The Times of India, Sept, 5, 2011.
11. Excerpts taken from "The New Indian Express" dated 26 August, 2011.

Odisha and Microfinance Initiatives

Odisha, along the eastern sea-bed of India is the home to nearly 41.9 million people. It has a glorious and ancient history spanning a period of over 2000 years. In ancient times, it was the proud kingdom of Kalinga. Kalinga was a major seafaring nation that controlled most of the sea routes in the Bay of Bengal. For several centuries, a substantial part of Southeast Asia, such as Kampuchea (Cambodia), Java, Sumatra, Bali and Thailand were its colonies. In fact, the name of the country "Siam" is derived from Oriya/Sanskrit Shyamadesha. The temple of Angkor Wat is a fine example of Oriya architecture, with some local variations. Bali still retains its Hindu Orissan heritage.

The economy of Odisha reflects a balanced mix of agricultural and industrial sectors.[12] As the apex industry body, Associated Chambers of Commerce and Industry of India (ASSOCHAM) Report has revealed in June, 2011, Odisha, over the last decade has registered 10.8 per cent growth rate, ahead of three other major provinces (Assam, Bihar and West Bengal) in eastern India. Besides, it has been stated as a bottom line province of the Indian Union. Its economy has registered an annual growth rate of 9.51 per cent during the 10th plan and 9.57 per cent in the first three years of the 11th Plan, notwithstanding the challenges posed by the global financial crisis. The per capita income of Odisha has registered a significant increase of 112.44 per cent during the period from 2004–05 to 2010–11. However, this rate of increase has proved to be less than that of the country, which has been as high as 120 per cent, according to

12. *Economic Survey, 2010–11, Planning and Coordination Department, Government of Odisha, Bhubaneswar.*

a Report placed before the Indian Parliament on 4th August, 2011[13].The higher growth in the economy in recent years has been contributed largely by the industrial sector followed by service sector. Though the share of agriculture sector in Gross State Domestic Product (GSDP) has been declining, the proportion of people dependent on agriculture has not been declining in the same proportion and rate.

According to the Economic Survey of Orissa, 2010–11, more than 60 per cent in Odisha still depends on the agriculture and allied sectors for their sustenance. For the last 3/4 years, The socio-economic fabric of the province has been disrupted by excessive Maoist activities. As the Survey Report puts, "the Provincial Government claimed reduction in poverty by 11.73 per cent between 2004–05 and 2007–08," the rural-urban poverty gap remaining larger than the National average. Besides, the coastal region has registered the sharpest decline of poverty according to 61st round of NSS (National Sample Survey). The extent of poverty in southern and northern regions is still very high and a matter of grave concern. It is also a fact that Odisha is prosperous in terms of huge mineral deposits underneath its soil, while witnessing abject poverty on top of its soil. Moreover, persistent Naxal activities result in a void in the socio-economic development of this region. Nevertheless, the need of the hour has been to put in extra effort for the economic development through a growing entrepreneurial class.[14] They need them for two reasons: to cash in on new opportunities and create wealth and new jobs.

13. The Dharitri, Bhubaneswar, 5th August, 2011.
14. *Behera, B. and Behera, S., "Entrepreneurship and Employment Opportunities in Odisha with Special Reference to Tourism", Published Paper, 3rd Biennial Center for ESBM International Conference, Jan. 22-23, 2011.*

Furthermore, Odisha has failed to come up to the expectation in developing small, medium and tiny industries. Thus, its Government has formulated a policy in the year 2009 for the development of medium, small and tiny industries. Its Government is all set to create a special fund for development of these enterprises in PPP (Private People Participation) mode. It also, on the face of growing unemployment and lack of quality employees, expresses serious concern for not being able to optimally exploit the benefits out of its long run and very critical industrialization drives including that of POSCO, TATA and Vedanta. This would help create employment, promote export furthering industrialization. While the fund would be operational through the The State Financial Commission (SFC), Government of Odisha and other Foreign Institutional Investors (FIIs) will invest for the fund. Especially, this is aimed at developing all the areas on the way to reduce regional disparities.

In Odisha, however, a large number of public sector banks have shown dismal performance in terms of the priority sector lending. Their performance under the Annual Credit Plan (ACP), can hardly be satisfactory, while their lending to agriculture has been mere 20 per cent of the target fixed for the first quarter of the current 2011–12 fiscal. Besides, in the 124th State Level Bankers' Committee, held on 18th August, 2011, Chief Minister of Odisha has pointed out that the per capita credit has been only 39 per cent of the national average[15]. Furthermore, MF as an effective form of poverty alleviation has made significant turn over in the years under review, i.e., 2008–09 and 2009–10. MF, the provision of financial services to low income clients aims at saving the life of people from the clutches of village moneylenders lending at

15. The New Indian Express, Bhubaneswar, Dated 19th August, 2011.

exorbitant rates of interest. Strikingly, SHGs/JLGs and their members are making exemplary contribution throughout the country. In the name of Rosani Yojana implemented since 2009, the President's Estate is provided with a novel approach of conserving energy through Solar power, utilizing garbage converted compost in the Estate collected from the home-makers and SHG members utilising unwanted torn paper in making usable articles. Recently, SHG groups in Odisha, have been assigned the task of providing mid-day meals for the school children, while 156 groups in its Nayagarh district are collecting electricity dues on behalf of the Central Electricity Supply Utility (CESU).

The Case of Adhikar and PF

Adhikar   Adhikar (literally meaning 'right') has been set up in 1991 by a group of young activist volunteers committed to the cause of protecting human rights of the poor in Odisha. It endeavours to prove as one of the leading institutions in Odisha in livelihood promotion dove-tailed into MF services. While undertaking a multitude of activities, it has the motive to serve the community towards its integrated development through the process of women empowerment. Its developmental initiatives include mobilization of a number of SHGs into Primary Self-help Co-operatives, creation of a secondary co-operative under The Orissa State Self-Help Co-operative Act, 2001, financial inclusion of the BPL families under Joint Liability Group (JLG) model and a remittance programme for the migrant people. Its MF initiatives have covered 15 districts in three states with the help of 40 branches.

Since its inception, Adhikar has been involved in promoting SHGs. To include maximum house holds in the process of financial inclusion, the organization launched the MF programme in the form of JLG in 2004. In the recent past, a Non-Banking Finance Company (NBFC) has been formed under the name Adhikar Microfinance Co. Ltd. This legal entity has helped boosting the confidence level of Adhikar in order to expand its activities to the neighbouring provinces like Andhra Pradesh and Gujarat. Moreover, the expansion of its activities to districts of Kalahandi, Bolangir and Koraput, popularly known as the KBK region have been need based.

People's forum   People's Forum is a 21-year-old development organization based in Odisha. Founded by few young students, PF is a non-profit and an apolitical organization. According to its Annual Reports, it has been working for sustainable development of the rural folks in order to strengthen the rural economy and effectively utilize the rural resources. PF is promoting SHGs both directly and through network partners covering more than 7500 groups with more than 8500 clientele. Its MF initiative is designated as Mission Annapurna. Presently, PF operates in 15 districts of Odisha through its 26 branches and 5 sub-branches each having a minimum of 200 SHGs. MF in PF, however, aims at securing the economic independence and sustainability of the poor.

Performance Analysis of Adhikar and PF

Operational performance analysis Adhikar has been consistently evaluating its programme in terms of quality of services and affordability of charges. The addition in outreach and reduction of the cost has supported the programme to decrease the rates of interest. Without any compromise with the quality of the programme, Adhikar has been able to position itself as a fast growing MFI nationally. Furthermore, among the three categories of loans advanced by Adhikar, income generating loan, housing loan are provided with 10 per cent flat and 24 per cent reducing rates of interests respectively. Its innovative education loan also provides opportunities to empower the poor children through education. Besides, it is quite noteworthy that Adhikar has gained name and fame for its pioneering work of providing remittance service to the migrants of Odias across the country. In tune with the demands of such migrant workers, money remittance was initiated from Gandhigram to the source area where the organization has had intervention with various community development activities. The process, however, begins with receiving money at the place of work and delivery of the same to the dependants of the migrant workers at their doorsteps in 48 hours. A total sum of 7.9 crores has been remitted in terms of 22380 transactions in a period of six years.

Among the few thrust areas of PF, it provides credit to SHGs linked with various banks. The performance of PF in respect of its lending has shown that agricultural loan, loan for petty business and microenterprises constitute 67 per cent, 16 percent and 17 per cent respectively. It offers attractive credit products in terms of accessibility, simplicity, and timely delivery while offering suitable loan periods and sizes. Moreover, the organization mobilizes its own resources, providing safe and attractive returns on the savings promoting voluntary withdrawal and providing doorstep collection services. It offers suitable products, e.g., passbook savings, fixed deposits and savings certificates. In order to ensure proper pricing, PF also covers its costs from the margin by setting appropriate interest rates at all levels of institutions involved. It, however, covers the cost of funds, administrative costs, loan losses and allows for a profit margin. The organization takes inflation into account while offering attractive real returns on savings.

Table 1   Credit Operations by Adhikar and PFF

Loan Type	Cycle		Tenure (In Months)		Amount (in thousand ₹)		Rate of Interest		Guarantee
	Adhikar	PF	Adhikar	PF	Adhikar	PF	Adhikar (Flat)	PF (Reducing)	Adhikar and PF
Income Generation	1st Cycle				7	8.3	10	15	GROUP
	2nd Cycle+				10	9.5	10	18	
	3rd Cycle			12–18	15	11	10	24	
	4th Cycle		12	36–60	20	10	10	24	
Housing Loan	Once		28					24	
Education Loan	Once		6		2-5		Nil		Relevant Documents

Source: The Annual Reports of Adhikar and PF

Table 2   Operational Performance of Adhikar and PF

Particulars (in numbers)	As on 31.03.2009		As on 31.03.2010	
	Adhikar	**PF**	**Adhikar**	**PF**
SHGs	15493	6693	18280	7065
Districts Covered	13	15	15	15
Beneficiaries	70354	81890	82728	87868
Loanee members	53859	36002	61742	46865
Staff supporting MF	160	102	162	102
Branches	35	22	40	35

Mangement Information System   Adhikar by playing a formidable role as an MFI in Odisha and elsewhere has been able to overcome its lapses with strict monitoring mechanism, computerized MIS and with stringent internal-external audit system. PF also practises the manual record keeping and data processing. Auditors are engaged to keep such financial records. However, the effort is on to develop a suitable MF software package to introduce software base on the system.

Client-Support Services   Adhikar makes continuous interaction and consultations with the officials looking into the co-operative activities at the district and the state level for sensitizing them and generating positive response in order to create a favourable climate for promotion of self-help co-operatives under The Self-Help Co-operative Act, 2001. Continuous counseling and mobilization processes are going on with different NGOs, Community-based Organisations (CBO) and SHGs in their operational area.

PF, on the other hand, has earned cooperation with like-minded agencies to provide add-on services in its operational areas. It has shaped a long term professional relationship with government organizations, NGOs and SHG Federations. For service sustainability, the organization has established service centers. PF has presently a microfinance staff of 102 with 99 volunteers who are responsible for promotion, management and tracking of SHGs as well as their credit utilization. While believing in result oriented works, it recruits and trains good staff providing them with training, skill and motivation along with practical exposure.

Financial performance analysis As it is revealed from Table 3, the financial indicators reflect a mixed performance in case of both the organizations. On all counts except the loans to women members in the year, 2009–10, Adhikar exhibits comparatively a better picture than PF. In the period under comparision between both the MFIs, general, fund in case of Adhikar is found to be safer than PF. But the former has reduced its PLL over the period, while the latter has increased the same.

However, both have increased their investment in fixed asset adding strength to their existence, whereas PF has put enough funds towards its loan for the women members in contrast to a fall in case of its counterpart, Adhikar. This may be attributed to the fact that the NBFC status received later by PF in the year, 2009–10 has prompted it to advance more loans to its women beneficiaries.

Table 3 Financial Performance of Adhikar and PF (in lakhs ₹)

Particulars	2008–09		2009–10	
	Adhikar	**PF**	**Adhikar**	**PF**
General Fund	23.12	6.55	31.79	22.19
Excess of Income over expenditure	9.52	6.54	12.06	5.90
Provision for loan loss (PLL)	6.00	0.04	4.53	2.20
Fixed assets	7.30	3.72	11.90	6.50
Loan advanced to women members	314.88	87.54	228.31	238.49

Source: Same as Table 1

Women Empowerment

Women Empowerment is defined as the processes, by which women take control and ownership of their lives through expansion of their choices. It also enables them to define goals and act upon them, and be aware of gendered power structures, self-esteem and self-confidence. Undeniably, women have incredible strength and endurance and can express life in countless colors, fields and subject. Adhikar and PF as well have given women a special attention. Focusing on their socio-economic upliftment, most of the SHGs/ JLGs associated with the two MFIs are women based. Often family members of these women are encouraged to take decisions based on their experience during entrepreneurship development and various capacity building programs. PF has also set up both a family counseling centre and helpline in

Mao-infested district of Malkangiri in order to solve cases related to family disturbances, domestic violence, marital conflicts, etc. On similar lines, Adhikar has been running a legal aid counseling centre to provide relief to the victims who are not in a position to get legal services easily. However, the following objectives have been laid down by the MFIs for the cause of women empowerment.

a. To ensure the socio-economic status of the women.

b. To create awareness among the women about their rights and privileges.

c. To protect them against domestic violence and groom them to live with self-respect and self-dignity.

Besides, both provide a wider range of MF services in order to improve ability of more than a lakh of poor women.

CONCLUSION

SMEs are a major contributor to the GDP of any country in general and developing countries in particular. They are even larger contributor to exports and employment. Their role gets magnified in a developing country like India, where they are the catalysts of growth with significant contribution to the manufacturing and service sector. This paper while presenting an SL approach in the context of enterprise, particularly, MSE development, aims at summarising the lessons learnt and insights gained from conducting SL research on the poor communities in Odisha for whom MSE activities has been a key component in case of their livelihood. As revealed by the foregoing discussion, credit being a powerful development tool, its effectiveness depends on its use. Again, the most important element of a credit institution while working with the MSE/informal sector is to demonstrate that the credit to this sector is financially viable. Without honest and sincere effort, credit cannot by itself resolve all of the structural and functional problems.

Here, it is worth mentioning that the literature available on the impact of SHG-based microcredit programmes demonstrates, "The groups maintain a high degree of solidarity, while practicing a culture of self-help and self-management. An MF programme can prove to be a magic wand only when it adopts accountability, transparency and the firm determination to eradicate poverty." Further, SHGs/JLGs have features, such as non-collateral loans and mutual guarantee in the group. Also, there exists a "financial gap", not covered by both the financial systems already discussed. Undoubtedly, the enterprises, which belong to this gap, have a potential to grow and create employment, even though they are small in size. Confronting the difficulties in raising funds from commercial banks, they also face a dilemma in that MF loans are not enough to meet their capital demand. As a result, they are forced to raise funds from informal finance such as the loans shark or relatives borrowings. On assessing the effectiveness of MF loans, the results indicate that majority of the borrowers have a tendency to misutilise the funds borrowed. They treat MF funding as just another source for meeting personal expenses. The research has identified this as serious concern for the Institutions, like Adhikar and PF dealing with MF activities.

In India, a rewarding feature of its economic development has, however, been the impressive growth of its entrepreneurs, particularly in modern small-scale industries (SSIs). Its rural economy has been subject to rapid technological advancements. Rural landscape in the country, inter alia, Odisha have started undergoing dramatic changes in terms of road connectivity, electrification, data connectivity. For millions, low-end mobile phones have proved to be a boon. Financial inclusion has been easier due to mobile as well as core banking. They have democratized communication and empowered the underclass. Yet, the bottleneck behind inclusive finance revolution has been the lack of financial awareness among the people mostly in rural areas.

Under these adverse circumstances, Adhikar and PF have been reasonably successful while rendering MF services over the last decades. As earlier mentioned, they have been instrumental in promoting women SHGs to be an effective vehicle for transformation of developmental ideas and effective tool for programme implementation. Various SHGs/JLGs intermediated by Adhikar and PF while showing positive impacts have played important roles in reducing the vulnerability of the poor women through asset creation, provision of emergency assistance and above all women empowerment. Both the MFIs are intervening in the semi-urban and rural economies of Odisha through their poverty intervention (MF) programs. In Odisha, growing unemployment, particularly the phenomenon of educated unemployment, has been persistently one of the baffling problems. With a rural population of approximately 85 per cent, the funding activity in Odisha has picked up few years back but there is lack of proper training to the MF beneficiaries.

Finally, it is evident from the various assessments mode that credit is a condition that is necessary, though it is not sufficient for the development and transformation of small-scale informal production. Thus, a credit programme, like MF need to be designed keeping in mind the needs, aspirations, skills and the existing social, economic, cultural and political system. The issues which contribute to the success of micro enterprise and MF in India vis-a vis Odisha has been analysed. Adhikar and PF have also made long strides since their inceptions through the SHG/JLGSs for women-driven community development. According to the study, given time and support, women can do wonders with their pious service orientation. In Odisha, their magic hands have been borrowed through the SHGs in programs like Mid-Day Meal, micro-farming, Public Distribution, etc. Moreover, the impressive role of the MFIs in question to promote SHGs among the poor while providing financial services offers opportunities to the beneficiaries through the novel SL approach. It is expected that analyses like these would eventually reveal the application of the entrepreneurial mindset development model in MFI-like organizations, in relation to the viability of small/micro businesses and their growth strategies.

References

1. Aghion, P. and P. Howitt, (1992) A Model of Growth through Creative Destruction.

2. Alesina, A. and D. Rodrik, (1994), "Distributive Policies and Economic Growth."

3. Annual Reports of Adhikar and People's Forum, 2007-08, 2008-09 and 2009-10.

4. Cahn Miranda (2006), "Sustainable Rural Livelihoods, Micro Enterprise and Culture in the Pacific Isands: Case Studies From Samoa, A Ph.D. Thesis, Massey University, New Zealand.

5. David H. Holt, (2008), Entrepreneurship, Prentice-Hall of India Pvt. Ltd., New Delhi

6. Desai, V,. (1992), "Dynamics of Entrepreneurial Development and Management", Himalaya Publishing House, Bombay.

7. Government of Orissa, "Economic Survey", 2009-10 and 2010-11

8. Hari Srinivas-hsrinivas@gdrc. Org

9. Khanka, S.S., (1999), "Entrepreneurial Development", S. Chand & Co. Ltd., New Delhi

10. Mahendra S. Dev, (2007), "Inclusive Growth in India ", Oxford University Press, New Delhi

11. Meher, S. (2003), SHGs and Poverty in Odisha, Nabakrushna Chaudhury Centre for Development Studies, Bhubaneswar.

12. Mike Albu and Andrew Scott, Intermediate Technical Development Group, November, 2001

13. M. N. Srinivas, (1980), India Social Structure, Hindustan Publishing Corporation, Delhi

14. Orissa Development Report (2003), Planning Commission, India.

15. Sehgal, G., "Microfinance for Small and Medium Enterprises: Prospects, Challenges and Implications", International Journal of Research in Commerce, Economics and Management, Vol. No. 1 (2011), Issue No.4

16. The IDBI and Micro Enterprise-Promoting Growth with Equity

17. Various News Paper Clippings

18. www.Livelihoodtechnology.org.

19. Yadav, S., (2010), Reservation and Inclusive Growth, Theme Paper for the 54th Members' Annual Conference, Indian Institute of Public Administration, New Delhi

9

ENTREPRENEURSHIP AND ENVIRONMENT

MEANING OF ENVIRONMENT

Entrepreneurship demands an enabling environment in order to flourish. "Environment", as the term defined by P. Gisbert suggests anything immediately surrounding an object and exerting a direct influence on it. According to Kimball Young, environment refers to "those forces, situations, stimuli which influence the organism from outside". The environment is more than a 'conditioning' factor of life. As aptly said by Maclver, "It interpenetrates life everywhere. It directs or diverts, stimulates and depresses man's energies. It moulds his speech, it subtly changes his frame. Nay, more it lives within him. It is entirely inescapable from life". However, environment varies greatly from one region to another. It may be favourable to business growth, or it may be hostile. The Oxford English Dictionary gives the meaning of the word "Environment" as surrounding objects, regions or circumstances. Environment implies every thing that is external to the organization

The nature of entrepreneurial activity that takes place in a particular community, state or nation is largely determined by the attitudes, beliefs, and needs of the particular locality. Sometimes, conversely, the entrepreneur's activity help to shape and direct life within the community. Business makes demands on society, and society makes demands on business. The sum of these interrelationships between business and the community comprise the business environment. Environment consists of the actors and factors external to the enterprise. It is the sum total of external factors within which the enterprise operates. It is made of tangible and intangible factors both controllable and uncontrollable. Environmental forces are depicted in the following diagram:

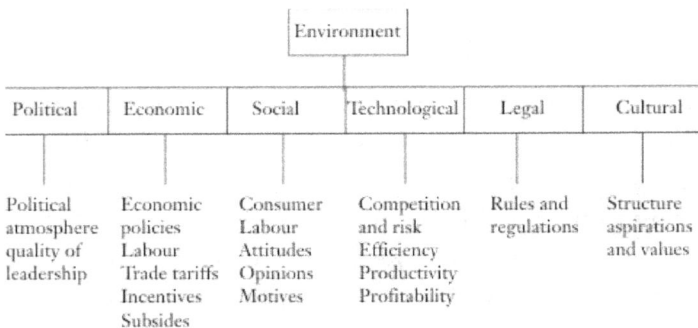

			Environment		
Political	Economic	Social	Technological	Legal	Cultural
Political atmosphere quality of leadership	Economic policies Labour Trade tariffs Incentives Subsides	Consumer Labour Attitudes Opinions Motives	Competition and risk Efficiency Productivity Profitability	Rules and regulations	Structure aspirations and values

Figure 9.1   Entrepreneunial Environment

Modern industry has provided a material prosperity unequalled in the human history. It has also created unparalleled environmental threats to the present and future generations alike. The very technology that has enabled to manipulate and control nature has polluted the environment and rapidly depleted the existing stock of natural resources. Although the nations have made significant progress in controlling certain types of pollution and in conserving energy, significant environmental trends are shaping the future of civilizations. This includes population growth, rising temperature, falling water tables, collapsing fisheries, shrinking forests and per capita crop land, and the loss of animal and plant species. The modest temperature rise in recent decades is melting ice caps and glaciers. Ice cover is shrinking in the Arctic, the Antarctic, Alaska, Greenland, the Alps, the Andes and the Quinghai-Tibetan Plateau. Forests, too are being overwhelmed by human demands. Over the past half-century and more, forested area in the world has shrunk substantially, with much of the loss occurring in developing countries like India. In some ways, the trend that will most affect the human prospect is an irreversible one—the increasing extinction of plant and animal species. According to some observers, the problems raised by these environmental threats are so intractable and difficult that they cannot be solved.

Entrepreneurship does not emerge and grow spontaneously. Rather it is dependent upon several economic, social, political and legal factors. An entrepreneur should understand the behaviour of the key environmental forces that have an implication on the enterprise and understand and get a grasp of the techniques available for environmental scanning. Last decade witnessed many of the industry titans losing their competitive advantage to relatively new entrants. For example, Hindustan Motors and Premier Automobiles Mahindra lost their pre-eminent position in the Indian market to Maruti Udyog Ltd. HMT lost their market to Titan, HLL's

Surf was cornered by Nirma, television giants Crown, Bush, Weston, etc. lost to ONIDA, BPL, etc. All these cases, and likewise many others explain that, sensitivity to the external environment consists of identification of opportunities and threats and tracing it to a particular source.

1. Political and Government forces

Government all over the world are important aspect of their economy. It is the government that regulated the business activities as it is the custodian of the nation. In fact, what is to be produced? how much? of what quality? for whom? when? and at what cost and at what price are to be determined by the policies of the government. The producers and marketers are to work within these concessions and limits set by political forces. Thus, government policies regarding pricing, fiscal, and regional preferential policies all have to be studied and interpreted before setting up the enterprise.

2. Economic Forces

Economic environment affects the demand structure of any industry/product. Markets require purchasing power. Purchasing power is a function of current income, prices, savings, and credit availability. Entrepreneurs should be aware of main trends in the economic environment, viz.,

- Gross national product
- Real per capital income
- Balance of payment position
- Trade cycles
- Trends in the prices of goods and services
- Fiscal policies and rate of interest

- Changing consumer expenditure pattern, etc.

Each of these may be an opportunity or threat to an enterprise. Changes in such major economic variables such as money income, cost of living, interest rate and savings and borrowing patterns have an immediate impact on the enterprise.

3. Social Forces

Structure of a society may be viewed as the attitudes that prevail in a society towards its many institutions, business, for example. The legal framework, the economic system and the state of technological development are each important considerations. But the ultimate design and consequently the impact of these factors depends on the attitudes of society. These attitudes depend in large measure on whether business has been responsive to the societal needs. This has been essentially true of the US since the great depression of the 1930s. The 19th century attitude towards business was based on the concept of personal leadership in businees affairs, on small-scale operation and on skilled workers. The early 20th century brought with it the concept of professional managerial services in very large-scale operation involving a high degree of mechanization and an impersonal relation between business and the labour force.

The society in which the people grow, shapes their basic beliefs, values and norms. Social factors in a country determine the extent and level of industrialization, as they influence the demand for a product or service at any given point of time. Changes in social forces refer to,

1. demographic changes and

2. geographical location changes.

An entrepreneur is required to understand the age composition which will help him in deciding optimal marketing mix, sex structure and the changing role of women and occupation and literacy profiles of the population. The study will help the entrepreneur to decide the product mix. For example, today 85% of Indian market is a young market; it is but natural for entrepreneurs to develop their markets for this group. A look at Indian population statistics reveal that women constitute 50% of total population and there is an increase in the number of working women especially in the urban and metrocities. This obviously requires many time saving appliances like cooking range, the pressure cooker, the washing machine, the vacuum cleaner, etc.

In addition to the above, an entrepreneur has to look for geographical shifts in the population. Another factor to look for in the social changes is the changes in the value system. Values are the beliefs which are held in the society. These are bound to have deep influence on consumer taste, temperament, life and living.

It goes without saying that an alert entrepreneur cannot afford to neglect or under-estimate these aspects.

4. Technological Forces

The most dynamic force, shaping people's destiny is technology. Technology has released such owners such as pencillin, birth control pill, x-ray, compact discs (CDs), etc. It has also released such horrors as nuclear bombs, submarine guns, etc. Every new technology is a force for creative destruction, e.g., television hurt cinemas.

An entrepreneur has to watch the trends in technology. The level of technological development in the industry creates an opportunity for an entrepreneur to develop new products. However, technological developments are greatly influenced by government policies and response of the industries in terms of investment in Research and Development. New technology will mean new ideas, new products and new marketing efforts. This requires the entrepreneur to keep an eye on fast changing technology.

If the last decade just ended was indicative of how technology can change our lives, the decade that is on the horizon is set to make technology accessible across the spectrum. With connectivity as the mantra, the digital divide between have's and have nots could soon be a thing of the past. Leading the change is the revolution in mobile telephony that has been responsible for connecting people on an unprecedented scale. From being a status symbol to a ubiquitous tool of personal convenience, the journey has indeed been a significant one. With smart phones becoming progressively cheaper, mobile telephony is set to transform our lives in ways that we would have imagined a decade ago.

5. Legal Forces

Entrepreneurial decisions are highly affected by the developments in the legal environment. This is made up of laws, government agencies and pressure groups that influence and constrain various organization and individuals in society. Legislation affecting business has steadily increased over the years. Every legislation ha a number of purposes. The first is to protect entrepreneurs from each other, the second purpose is to protect consumer from unfair business practices and thirdly it is to protect the larger interest of society against mischievous business society. An entrepreneur needs a good knowledge of the major laws protecting competition, consumer and larger interest of the society. Entrepreneur should not only know the laws but also realize the role of laws in the organized society. There are certain regulations which lay down procedures for obtaining import license, raw material permits, financial assistance and foreign exchange permits and entrepreneurs should have at least a working knowledge of these formalities.

6. Cultural Forces

People in a given society hold many core beliefs and values that will tend to persist. Core beliefs and values are passed on from parents to children and are reinforced by the major institutions of society, schools, temples, business and government. People's secondary beliefs and values are more open to change. Each culture has sub-culture. Secondary cultural values undergo shifts through time. Entrepreneurs should have a keen interest in anticipating cultural shifts in order to spot new entrepreneurial opportunities or threats.

7. Physical Forces

Entrepreneurs should be aware of pros and cons of opportunities combined with the availability of physical resources, i.e., raw materials. The Earth's materials consists of,

    i.   An infinite resource such as air and water,

    ii.   Finite renewable resources such as food and forests but these are to be used wisely,

    iii.   Finite nonrenewable resources such as oil, coal and minerals.

Entrepreneurs should have a constant watch on the availability of above physical resources and tune their manufacturing activities.

It is a cliché, but it is true—things are changing rapidly around us. In such an environment, one needs an understanding of the forces that shape a domain—technogy or business—so that one is able to anticipate changes. One needs to avail rigorous data-oriented approach for creating scenarios. One must design for the future. To be one step ahead of the curve, one needs the confidence to extrapolate the curve. That is what is done at Infosys. That is the reason, powered by intellect and driven by values, Infosys is the face of new India.

A world leader in consulting and IT services, Infosys partners with Global 2000 companies to provide business consulting, systems integration, application development and product engineering services. Through these services Infosys enables its clients to exploit technology for a complete business transformation. Its approach focuses on new ways of business that combine IT innovation and adoption while also leveraging on organisation's current IT assets. Infosys works with large global corporations and next-generation technology companies, to implement prudent business and technology strategies in today's dynamic digital environment.

Thus, an information about environment is necessary for the successful conduct of the business activities. Environment opens up fresh avenues for the expansion of new entrepreneurial activities. The entrepreneurs may come forward with new ideas and with new ventures when they find environment suitable to their enterprises and advantageous to them. An acquisition of knowledge about the changing environment will keep entrepreneurs dynamic in their approach which helps the business to avoid ecological problems and maintains harmony with business environment. The entrepreneur should study the nature and character of control over the enterprise exercised by the environment, and should try to adjust to the conditions prevailing and thus influence the environment in order to make it congenial and favourable to them.

Professor Agarwal in this connection wrote the penalty of environmental disregard is heavy. It not only reduces profit margins and makes opportunities for expansions, but it also arouses social hostility and makes social environment growingly inhospitable to business operations. A deep knowledge of the environment is the way to succeed in any sphere ranging from self-employment to the other services.

CONCLUSION

In conclusion, economic growth and environment encompassing several issues need to be addressed at the right tme and in right perspective. While the environment in general receives adequate attention from across the world, India among other things takes proactive steps recognizing the needs to champion green causes in a big way. However, the issue is whether, as a developing nation on a high trajectory growth path, India can afford to view environment and development as anything but mutually reinforcing categories.

10

CULTURE CAREER AND COMPETENCE

INTRODUCTION

The term 'Culture' has varying definitions. "Culture, in its broadest definition, refers to that part of the total repertoire of human action (and its product) which is socially, as opposed to genetically, transmitted." Man is not only social but also cultural. It is the culture that provides opportunities for man to develop the personality. Development of personality is not an automatic process. Every society prescribes its own ways and means of giving social training to its new born members so that they may develop their own personality. For the individual, culture has got a great value. It forms an important element in his social life. It is culture that makes the human animal a man, regulates his conduct and prepares him for his group life. Culture is preserved, diffused and transmitted by conscious efforts of the group. It has given new vision of life. It assimilates, adopts, creates new needs and new drives and satisfies the asthetic, moral and religious interests of the members of the group. In short, culture is the expression of finer aspect of the lifestyle of a group. In this sense, the literature, art, architecture, music, dance, drama, food, clothing, festivals, philosophy and religion, etc., reflect culture of a group.

A very popular definition is that of Edward Burnett Taylor, "Culture of civilization is that complex whole which includes knowledge, belief, art, morals, law, custom, and other capabilities and habits acquired by man as a member of society." Clyde Kluckhohn has defined culture very simply as "the total life or way of a people". When the concept first emerged in eighteenth and nineteenth century Europe, it refered to a process of cultivation or improvement, as in agriculture and horticulture. In the nineteenth century, it came to refer first to the betterment or refinement of the individual, especially through education and fulfilment of national aspirations. However, in the mid-nineteenth century, some scientists used the term "culture" to refer to a universal human capacity. For the German non-positivist sociologist, George Simel, culture referred to "the cultivation of individuals through the agency of external forms which have been objectified in the course of history".

In the twentieth century, "culture" emerged as a concept central to Anthropology, encompassing all human phenomena that are not purely results of human genetics. Specifically, the term "culture" in American anthropology had two meanings:

(1) the evolved human capacity to classify and represent experiences with symbols and to act imaginatively and creatively; and

(2) the distinct ways that people living in different parts of the world classified and represented their experiences.

The concept of culture is used to distinguisn human societies from animal groups. The customs, ideas, and attitudes shared by a group, which make up its culture are transmitted from generation to generation by learning processes rather than biological inheritance. Adherence to these customs and attitudes is regulated by systems of rewards and punishments peculiar to each culture. Languge and other symbolic media are the chief agents of culture transmission, but many behaviour patterns are acquired through experience alone. A pattern of cultural universals is found in all societies. It includes such human institutions as social organisation, and material culture (tools, weapons, and clothing). Societies are differentiated according to the degree of complexity of cultural organisation. Basically, each human group has its own distinctive culture, but a complex society may have sub-cultures determined by national origin, religion or social status. The spread of culture traits through direct or indirect contact among groups is called diffusion. A culture area is the territory within which a certain configuration of culture traits is to be found.

Many innovations have transformed the society and altered our pattern of living and many services have been introduced to alter or create new service industries. India vis-à-vis Odisha needs entrepreneurs. They need them for two reasons: First, to cash in on new opportunities and second to create wealth and new jobs. According to an estimate of a report by Mckinsey & Company-Nasscom, 110–130 million citizens in India will be searching for jobs by 2015, including 80–100 million looking for their first jobs than seven times of Australia's population. This does not include disguised unemployment of over 50 per cent among 230 million employed in rural India. Since traditional large employers, including the government and the old economy players may find it difficult to sustain this level of employment in the future, it is the role of the entrepreneurs to create these new jobs and opportunities.

CAREER

A very common question in the minds of young educated individuals arises as to which career to choose, after the completion of education. This is the most crucial moment in an individual's life, after the individual steps out from the college or university, and chooses a career. The choice that the individual makes at that point of time determines the remaining part of his /her life. If one's career choice is right, chances of success is big. If not, there is probability of failure and a lifelong struggle. In fact, most of the individuals during their study dream to become successful IT engineers, scientists, bureaucrats or doctors. Many are also guided by the wishes of their parents or superiors thus being able to build a secure career.

It is equally true that success and failure alike are the two sides of the same coin. Since everybody does not possess the right aptitude, it may amount to one's frustration. Sometimes, after many unsuccessful attempts for clearing competitive examinations, some individuals are forced to take up jobs they may not like. But, the individual would be pursued to choose something else, if he or she is not fit for that particular profession. In the contemporary social environment of India, selecting a right career is difficult as a variety of career counselling and suggestions are found from different sources. All these sources, however, do not prove to be objective and purposeful as well. More often than not, they may result in making wrong career decisions.

Inner Strength and Decision-Making

Inherent strengths and weaknesses are the factors that need to be diagnosed through self-introspection. Self-assessment can reveal one's inner potential. This assessment can very well be done by talking to successful persons, observing own reactions at the times of distress and comparing self-achievements with the achievements of the group to which one belongs. This self-analysis can develop the confidence and aptitude. Thus, knowing one's value is very important to prepare, adjust and sustain in a career. Further, a self-analysis provides one with a deep and fruitful insight into hidden potentials, strengths and weaknesses that would help an individual in exercising a career option. The strengths include educational and professional qualifications, experience, ability to convince people, business acumen and aptitude, capacity to get the result, etc. Similarly, the weaknesses can be viewed in terms of qualifications, lack of experience and confidence, lack of confidence in dealing with people, etc. An objective analysis, however, will ensure a proper direction to one's career.

Choosing and managing a career requires serious thinking and decision-making. First among all is the question of aptitude. Aptitude is considered to be one of the indicators for someone's success. Also, it should be remebered that everyone's life is a product of the choices that one makes. One among such choices is that of a career. Next factor happens to be commitment and measuring one's capabilities. It is necessary to be honest with your self and assess the kind of time that you can put in and the resources at your disposal.

General Awareness

A sharp mind with a detailed knowledge of the environment is the way to succeed in any sphere ranging from self-employment to the other services. This is an important factor that one must be absolutely sure about himself/herself fom both technical and professional point of view. Besides, general awareness about environmental variables is a must. However, such awareness can never be possessed overnight. In case of self-employment, a person well conversant with the environment has a chance to succeed. Further, one who is confident of addressing an issue and taking on the challenges of life is always ahead above others.

Professionalism

'Professional' according to its dictionary meaning has two implications. The first, one is related to job or profession. The second, meaning means well-trained or a person who is good at one's work. It is always better to shoulder any responsibility with passion rather than doing anything without it. They are simple examples of professional and non-professional behaviour. Moreover, this is the age while everybody desires to be a professional or to have an assignment in a professionally managed environment/organisation.

A Case of Video Editing as a career

Editing is considered to be a profitable career opportunity for the video people these days, particularly the educated youth. People who wish to pursue their career in media and entertainment have taken to video editing as one among the best for the creative ones. Selecting this as a career is, no doubt an interesting and challenging option as well. In this field, one need not have any specific educational qualification. As this is a very competitive field, people must be ready to accept challenge coupled with risk. Video editors must always be alert possessing up to date knoweldge to be equipped with the advanced technique in the field. Generally, the job of a video editor involves computer systems along with the knowledge of computer editing software and digital camera technology.

Freelance assignment of video editing is, in fact, very popular. While gone are the days of video editors to work on the site as that of a cameraman/photographer, with the appropriate skill and own editing system (computer), one can undertake video editing at one's comfortable time and from one's own home. This fact suggests that one need not necessarily search for a local assignment/job in video editing, he can work as a freelancer anywhere of his/her choice. This profession requires a lot of creative input. One's ability to get the job done on time and to the client's specification are considered much greater than one's ambition based upon creativity.

Ajit Jain—Indian-born looking at The career of Buffett

Jain was born in 1951, in Orissa. He graduated from IIT-Kharagpur in 1972 with a bachelor's degree in mechanical engineering. After working in IBM, India between 1973 and 1976, he moved to the US, where he did MBA from Harvard and joined Mckinsey & Co. He returned to India in the early eighties to get married. According to Robert P Miles', The Warren Buffett CEO: Secrets from the Berkshire Hathaway Managers, Jain confessed to his friends he would not have returned to the US, but for his wife who wanted to move there.

Jain specialises in mega-catastrophe coverage, that is, he takes risks that rivals avoid. For instance, he insured the Sears Tower in Chicago, America's tallest building, after the September 11, 2001 terrorist attack. He also underwrote the Winter Olympics at Salt Lake City in 2002, when big groups shunned the games as too risky after the attack. A Bloomberg report in 2006 said that after joining Berkshire, Jain placed advertisements in industry publications, which read something like: "We are looking for more—more casualty risks where the premium exceeds $1 million. The Berkshire Hathaway Insurance Group currently has $2 billion in surplus—that's right, $2 billion. And, because we retain the entire risk ourselves, instead of laying it off in the uncertain world of reinsurers, we have the flexibility to respond to your specific needs."

This was typical of Buffett's style of building Berkshire by saying: "Send us your deals", and then just answering the phone. In the last few years, there has been a lot of speculation about Buffett's succession. In dealing with it, Jain has shown that apart from his "extraordinary talent and discipline", he also shares with his boss an extraordinary sense of humour. Sample this: In an email response to a reporter who wanted to interview him on Berkshire's succession, Jain wrote: "It is undoubtedly the case that any disappointment I have caused you by declining the interview is far less than the disappointment I would have caused you by granting it."

COMPETENCE

When you see entrepreneurs, you find that some run their business successfully called 'successful entrepreneurs' while others fail. Then, a question arises: what makes the entrepreneurs successful. In other words, what are the characteristics or qualities of the successful entrepreneurs. The possession of certain knowledge, skill or personality profile called *'entrepreneurial competencies'* or *'traits'* help the entrepreneurs perform well. In the following section, an attempt has been made to explain the concept and development of entrepreneurial competencies or traits.

Meaning of Entrepreneurial Competency or Trait

In simple terms, a competence is an underlying characteristic of a person which leads to his/her effective or superior performance in an job. A job competence is a good combination of one's underlying characteristics such as one's knowledge, skill, motive, etc., which one uses to perform a given job well. It is important to mention that the existence of these underlying characteristics may or may not be known to the person concerned. This implies that the underlying characteristics may be unconscious aspects of the person. The underlying characteristics possessed by an entrepreneur which result in superior performance are called the entrepreneurial competencies or 'traits'.

In order to understand more and better about entrepreneurial competencies, let us first understand its components, i.e., knowledge, skill and motive. These are detailed out as follows.

What is Knowledge? In simple terms, knowledge means collection and retention of information in one's mind. Knowledge is necessary for performing a task but not sufficient. Let us explain this with an example. A person having the knowledge of playing cricket could be in a position to describe how to play. But, mere description will not enable the listener to play cricket unless something more than knowledge is there. We see in real life that people possessing mere knowledge have miserably failed while actually performing the task.

What this implies is that one also needs to have skills to translate the knowledge into action/practice.

What is Skill? Skill is the ability to demonstrate a system and sequence of behaviour which results in something observable, something that one can see. As put by Frederick Harbison, entrepreneurship implies the skill to build an organization. Building an organization requires lot of skills. A person with planning ability, i.e., skill, can properly identify the sequence of action to be performed to win a cricket match. Remember, while knowledge of playing cricket could be acquired by reading, talking or so on, skill to actually play cricket can be acquired by practice, i.e., by playing on a number of occasions. This means both knowledge and skill are required to perform a task.

Of late, soft skills have emerged as a tool with enough power to make or break one's career. Soft skill is an umbrella term which includes communicative skills, listening skills, team skills, leadership quality, creativity and logic, problem-solving skills and readiness to change among others. Soft skills are generally gifted. It cannot be learnt from a book. Still, formal training can, of course, give one fresh perspective and teach you tips and techniques if one needs to improve specific skills. If one really wants to in-gain soft skills into one's personality, he/ she must be a keen observer, an eager learner and an assiduous workman/woman religiously putting to practice all that one has learnt.

The case of Plumbing, A Crucial skill in the Construction Industry:

Plumbing as an important skill concerns public health. Though, a key segment of the construction industry, plumbing should not be treated as just another building service. It not only illustrates the dire conditions faced by those without accesst clean water and sanitation, but also makes a strong case for portable water and safe sanitation as a basic human right. In the developed countries, a plumber is considered as the health keeper to the nation. However, in India, he is the last man in the hierarchy. Despite a booming construction industry in the country, hardly there is implementation of plumbing codes and standards comparable to the world standards.. Onn the face of a dearth of trained workers, of late corporate houses such as Larson and Toubro have started their own skill training institutes.

What is Motive? In simple terms, motive is an urge to achieve one's goal what McClelland terms 'Achievement Motivation'. This continuous concern of goal achievement directs a person to perform better and better. Coming back to the same example of cricket playing, one's urge to become the best player helps him constantly practice playing to look out for ways and means to improving his performance.

Thus, in order to perform any task effectively and successfully including establishing and running an industrial unit, a person (entrepreneur) needs to possess a set of knowledge, skill and motive which could be together lebelled as 'competencies' or 'traits'.

MAJOR ENTREPRENEURIAL COMPETENCIES

More often than not, a controversy, however, surfaces as what it takes to be a successful entrepreneur. Earlier, people used to believe that entrepreneurs are born not made. Perhaps, persons with business as a family background could become successful entrepreneurs. Subsequently, the sharpened knowledge regarding entrepreneurial competencies over the last four decades made people believe that entrepreneurs are made, not born. According to this view, persons possessing proper knowledge and skill acquired through education and experience can become successful entrepreneurs. In view of the above controversy in order to understand clearly what it takes to be a successful entrepreneur, research institutions and behavioural scientists, through research, have tried to resolve the controversy on what makes a successful entrepreneur. Below, we present the findings of the representative institutional and individual research studies on entrepreneurial competencies.

Entrepreneurship Development Institute of India (EDI) Study

Entrepreneurship Development Institute of India (EDI), Ahmedabad, conducted a research study to identify what makes an entrepreneur successful. The study was conducted under the guidance of Professor David C. McClelland, a well-known behavioural scientist in three countries—of India, Malawi and Equador. The outcome of the study has been identification of entrepreneurial competencies or characteristics that result in superior performance. The major finding of the study was that the possession of competencies is necessary for superior performance. This was cross culturally valid.

Following is a list of major competencies identified by the study that lead to superior performance of the entrepreneurs:

1. **Initiative** It is entrepreneur who initiates a business activity.

2. **Looking for Opportunities** He looks for an opportunity and takes appropriate actions as and when it arises.

3. **Persistence** He follows the Japanese proverb "Fall seven times; stand up eight". He makes repeated efforts to overcome obstacles that get in the way of reaching goals.

4. **Information Seeker** Takes individual research and consults experts to get information to help reach the goal.

5. **Quality Conscious** Has a strong urge to excel to beat the existing standard.

6. **Committed to Work** Does every sacrifice to get the task completed.

7. **Efficiency Seeker** Makes always tenacious efforts to get the task completed within minimum costs and time.

8. **Proper Planning** Formulates realistic and proper plans and then executes rigorously to accomplish the task.

9. **Problem Solver** Always tries to find out ways and means to tide over the difficult times.

10. **Self-Confidence** A strong believer in his strengths and abilities.

11. **Assertive** Good in asserting his issues with others for the cause of his enterprise.

12. **Persuasive** Able to successfully persuade others to do what he actually wants from them.

....

13. **Efficient Monitor** Personally supervises the work so that employees have a lot of bargaining power in a sector where demand for certain skills is rising fast.

We, at least some of us, are good at self-goals. BPO/IT is India's calling card in global competitiveness assessments. Indian BPO/IT companies are now establishing centres elsewhere, even in Latin American countries where the notion of India headquartered multi-national operations would have been considered mad half-a-dozen years ago.

David Thomas

David Thomas who turned 40 in November, 2005, was smart, competent and fully devoted to his organization. A graduate from one of the Indian Institutes of Technology, he went on to get an MBA from one of the best management schools before starting his career with a leading Indian corporate. Somewhere during his career, he felt that he should be working for a multi-national organization (MNC), partly because of the lure of higher compensation along with the fact that just the smug words, 'works in an MNC' conveys that you are doing alright. That was then. Today, as he looks at the next 15–20 years of his life, David feels deeply troubled. He feels that he has leveled out. The work that he performed so well just a few years ago is no longer as consequential to the organization. There is something in the air that tells him that his career is festooned with autumn colours. Too many organizational changes to confuse him. How would he get a long-term career planned in the larger landscape of the huge organization? Indeed, he is at crossroads. What David can do today? Unfortunately, no one is telling him about it. However, he has an option to start his own and become an entrepreneur. Here is why: Entrepreneurs create jobs. Jobs provide people with livelihoods. Without a livelihood, everyone feels lost. There is an estimated 6.5 billion people on Earth. Out of this, a third lives right here in India and China. In the Indian sub-continent alone, there are 450 million children below 15, set to join the work force. It is neither for the government, nor for large businesses, to create avenues for employment and growth for these people. It can only be done by entrepreneurs. Entrepreneurs drive innovation. Finally, the world has become an entrepreneur-friendly place like never before. No government in the world says, "We do not like entrepreneurs". Funding for new ventures is becoming increasingly cross-border. Further, more resources are presently chasing fewer ideas, rather than the other way round. Consider breaking free to start on your own. It could well bring back the sheer feeling of exhillration when your first appointment letter was delivered in your youthful hands, a good 22 years back!

Well then, David Thomas, probably the time has come to shed your sense of being confused.

11

FRANCHISING AND ENTREPRENEURSHIP

INTRODUCTION

Challenges in the present century are very different from the past which require different approaches. Recent years have witnessed a cascading downturn in the world economy leading to tremendous decline in business and employment globally, particularly in the developed world. While the developed world was mauled by the meltdown of their economies, Indian economy only slowed down in maintaining its growth trajectory. The economy of India has remained largely unaffected by this recession, staying virtually at the same level as some of the most developed countries. This feat of survival from recession brings to the fore India's inherent strengths enabling it to face one of the worst economic crises of our time. In this context, the contemporary India has, in fact, an

204 Entrepreneurship Text and Cases

increasing need of entrepreneurs for two reasons: to cash in on new opportunities and create wealth and new jobs. According to an estimate of a report by Mckinsey & Company-Nasscom, 110–130 million citizens in India will be searching for jobs by 2015, including 80–100 million looking for their first jobs than seven times of Australia's population. This does not, however, include disguised unemployment of over 50 per cent among 230 million employed in rural India. Since traditional large employers may find it difficult to sustain this level of employment in the future, it is the role of entrepreneurs to create these new job opportunities.

Against this backdrop, franchising is always viewed by the potential entrepreneurs as one of the options for making a business. Gaining momentum recently, it has really enabled business people to carry on their business with minimum risk and without even much knowledge and experience in the world of business. Franchise can very well be considered as an alternative strategy for an entrepreneur to expand the business. Also as a marketing format, franchising has a lot of potential to grow, and those with even the basic business acumen can make profits galore.

MEANING AND DEFINITION

Franchising is the process of creating networks of business systems with consistent and repeatable operations. A franchise is a form of business ownership created by contrast whereby a company grants to a buyer the rights to engage in selling or distributing its products or services under a prescribed business format in exchange for royalty or shares of profits. According to D.H. Holt, franchising is defined as, "A business system created by a contract between a parent company called the franchisor, and the acquiring business owner, called the franchisee, giving the acquiring owner the right to sell goods or services, to use certain products, names, or brands, or to manufacture certain brands." The contract between the former and the latter is called a frachise agreement. Moreover, franchising can be considered from two dimensions. A small entrepreneur can consider buying a business as a franchisee, whereas, an innovative as well as successful entrepreneur can very well be a franchisor. Malls mostly selling shoes, toys, textile and photographic items are franchisees. Under a franchise agreement, manufacturer/sole distributor of a branded good/service, gives exclusive rights for distribution locally to the independent vendors with royalty and as per the agreed operating procedures.

Fundamentally, a contractual arrangement is made in which a franchisee enters into an agreement with a franchisor to sell the latter's goods/services for a specified fees/commission". A franchisor expands its business through a network of income-generating industrial/commercial units that share a common name, sell similar products, use common materials and receive the benefits out of integrated advertising and distribution systems. Franchise today, within its ambit, encompasses many industries. A franchise is a business system in the sense that it is capable of being replicated with consistent success.

THE RATIONALE AND RELEVANCE OF FRANCHISE AS A BUSINESS MODULE

Stunning changes have occurred in many industrial sectors. For instance, Red Carpet Realty opted into franchise business in 1977. Within next ten years, nearly a third of the home real estate business took the franchise route in the US. Also, in India, franchise is taken to be a promising sector with potentials to turn out many new entrepreneurs. A question may be put, "Have you always been someone daring to experiment with your entrepreneurial skills, and were put on the back foot because you thought brand building would be an expensive proposition? Then, being a franchisee for an already established product or service is just the right way to go?" In fact, India's economy has flourished so extensively that we have become a viable and beneficial destination for foreign franchisers. However, franchiser provides advertising and publicity support, key business practices and technical know-how. The legacy of franchising started with Issac Singer of Singer Sewing machines who wanted to increase distribution of the sewing machine. So he made efforts to set up franchising in the US. In that sense, he can be termed as a pioneer in franchising. Thereafter around 1919, food service establishments started franchising to gain momentum. With the development of inter-state High Way systems in 1950s, the US witnessed a simultaneous boom of franchise business in fast food restaurants, motels and dinners. McDonald's is among world's most successful restaurant chains.

When a company is looking out for expanding its business without investing in real estate as well as infrastructure, it can very well opt for franchising model for the same. For instance, Real Estate Bank India (REBI), conceived in February 2006, is an innovative emergence in the real estate arena with an ultimate aim of organising the unorganised sector in the present scenario. REBI's business mission is to create best value, value enhancing and value-based real estate organisation in the world by enabling customers to engage in property transactions, anywhere and anytime. REBI is setting up India's first national Organised Real Estate Transaction Network by means of appointing master franchisee, franchisees and Real Estate Transaction Advisers (RETAs) there.

Presently, there are over 70,000 franchisees, with an annual turnover of at least $4 billion, with over 4 lakh people directly employed in the franchised business. In Hyderabad, as the inhabitants of a multi-ethnic city, consumers have sufficient exposure to branded products laying the foundation for prosperous franchising.

Franchising/Agency/Dealership/ Distributorship

More often than not, the terms like franchising, agency, dealership and distributorship as well are assumed to carry the same meaning, whereas, they are different. In franchising, while a franchisor can enjoy greater control over the franchisee, in rest of the cases, the principal (producer) has no real control over the agent, dealer or distributor. However, these remaining forms of arrangements are, in fact, more traditional forms of distributing goods and services.

TYPES OF FRANCHISING

i. Product Franchise

It happens to be the oldest form of franchise business. Here, a franchisor gives right to distribute the trade-marked goods to a franchisee accepting a fee mutually agreed upon. This is found to be typical in both automobile and petroleum industries alike.

ii. Manufacturing Franchise

This type of business is characterised by soft drink industry. In this case, an arrangement is made whereby the franchisor gives the dealer the sole right to make as well as sell the product in a specified area.

iii. Business Format Franchise

Comparatively, this is of a recent origin. Being popular in the US, here a wide range of services are provided by the franchisor. On his part, it is mandatory to be interested in the franchisee's enterprise usually in areas like know-how, training. Whereas, the latter makes considerable investment on his own.

THE FRANCHISOR'S CONSIDERATIONS

An ideal franchise business benefits both the parties, i.e., the franchisor and the franchisee as well. While, successful franchising provides the income consistently, critical success factors in case of Red Carpet Realty and ComputerLand have seemingly been similar. They offered the consumers comprehensive service, consistency and quality performance. This led to expansion of their consumer base which, in turn, increased the demand for franchise locations. As a result, more franchise chains were created by a founding entrepreneur (e.g., Sarvana group of business organizations) in a single location.

Furthermore, mostly it is seen that entrepreneurs become franchisors either by way of conversion of some existing enterprise into chains or creation of new business concepts aimed at franchise style of business. For instance, Red Carpet Realty was a conversion by independent real estate broker who developed a service network under one name. However, ill-managed locations, inconsistent performance or overextended owners damage the entire network. Franchisors earn their income in the following ways:

1. *Start-up Fee*   Fee received initially is the single payment by the buyer to acquire the right from the franchisor. While giving the ownership rights, he offers a prepackaged business plan including vendor contracts, start-up

procedures along with operational guidelines. Besides, the initial fee covers a start-up programme with management training, assistance for site selection, accounting support and on-site consulting by the franchisor's personnel serving as the mentors to 'jump-start' the new business.

2. *Products and Supplies* For the stores dealing with patented or copy right goods/services, a franchisee is left with no choice of vendors. However, the benefits to the franchisee in case of the stores dealing with sports goods and computers include the rights of national-brand license, while the franchisor works with an established system of procurement. In fact, franchisor's strength reflects his ability to make bulk purchases, distribute efficiently, and guarantee quality.

3. *Royalty* The income derived out of sales is, indeed, the essence of franchise business. Usually, a royalty is fixed as a percentage of gross sales, though in some cases, fixed payment is determined on the volume of sales. In certain cases also, a flat fee is payble monthly. Some agreements of franchise replace royalty with percentage splits in the gross profit.

4. *Promotional Fees* As a part of the marketing programme of the franchisor, countrywide promotion and the fees for advertising are clearly mentioned in the franchise agreement. Accordingly, a franchisee uses to pay the company a monthly advertising fee on the basis of volume of gross sales. Further, additional fees are collected periodically for any joint promotional campaign.

5. *Services to Franchisees* Franchise agreements can specify few basic services to be provided by the franchisor for which they receive a retainer or periodic fee. They may include

book keeping, purchasing contracts, marketing research, legal assistance, maintenance, technical advertising and pay-roll accounting. Sometimes also, franchisors arrange leases on fixture and equipments besides providing credit collection and security assistance. Most of the services, are, however, pre-arranged in the basic agreement, while they are mostly negotiable.

6. *Real Estate Income*   Franchisors in cases like McDonald's and Jiffy Lube Garages build and lease new outlets that require unique physical facilities. In others like mail America service centres and the Foot locker stores making use of existing store fronts or mall locations, they are typically leased by the franchisee independently. While franchisors seldom get involved in mall leases, they regulate (occasionally providing finance) renovations and store fixtures.

7. *Franchisee* is the contractual owner of the proprietary business system with right to patent and copy right and branded products. Associated with a strong marketing plan given by the franchisor, the franchisee can start the business with few complications. As franchising requires uniformity as well as consistency, the franchisors give up autonomy in merchandising and purchase decisions. However, he must stick to the conditions in the agreement in order to restrict growth and limit potential to the capacity of a location. These limitations are overcome by the franchisees by buying additional outlets or expanding into a master franchise.

   A master franchisee is a contract that allows an entrepreneur to establish multiple locations within a defined geographical area. The parent organization awards an entrepreneur the right to be a regional franchisor who can contract independently. More often than not, frachisors offer master franchise options for selected regions, thereby leading to a form of regional management that diffuses distribution and decision-making control. Master franchises prove to be complicated arrangements between franchisors and other well-established business persons who possess resources to expand rapidly and manage growth. In the light of the above observations, it can be very well said that buying into a franchise requires careful and a detailed consideration.

CONCLUSION

Franchising tends to create networks of business systems with consistent and repetitive operations. For an individual owner buying into a business, franchising offers a comprehensive system of business based on a record of proven success. Though franchise business appears to be very attractive, it is not necessarily less expensive or more profitable than opening an independent venture. A proven marketing programme and an established business concept being offered by the franchisor, it may prove to be less risky. At the same time, the independent entrepreneur and his/her franchise counterparts have the similar operating needs. While, success always rests with the personal skills of an owner-operator, both the parties face the same long hours, managerial challenges and personal commitments.

In terms of buying into business, there are several differences between independent ventures and franchises. In case of acquiring a business, everything is negotiable, while the seller helps with some form of financing or equity assistance. On the other hand, there are fewer negotiable issues in case of franchise, the franchisor rarely gets involved in financial assistance beyond credit. Furthermore, the independent business man, can very well sell or assign the business and its assets, which is not possible for a franchisee due to the restrictions put as per the contractual arrangement.

REFERENCES

1. Donald D. Boroian and Patrick J. Boroian. The Franchise Advantage (Schaumburg, Il: National best Seller, 1987), PP.32-36.

2. David D. Seltz, How to Get Started in Your Own Franchised Business (Rockville Centre, NY: Farnsworth, 1980), PP.6–8.

3. Holt David H. (2008): Entrepreneurship Prentice Hall of India, New Delhi; P.465.

12

ENTREPRENUERIAL TEAM

BUILDING AN INSTITUTION

Now this is one where many entrepreneurs differ, even successful ones. There are some who treat it as mere wealth creation tools and there are others who believe in creating an institution that survives beyond them and leaves a legacy behind. Personally, the final and true glory of entrepreneurship lies in creating an institution that survives decades if not centuries. It redefines its market place, it becomes more than mere business. It becomes a way of life, a tradition; one that touches millions of lives across the globe or in a region. That is the final challenge which even successful ones stumble at with history as the only judge. However, by no means are these the complete list of challenges facing an entrepreneur.

Further entrepreneurship is the ability to build a founding team to complement entrepreneurial skills and talents. The success of an enterprise is more often determined by the individuals who lead it forward than by its products or services. The entrepreneurial team transforms creative ideas into commercial realities through their hard work and determination. A commonly used phrase by venture capitalists is that they prefer a grade A entrepreneurial team with a grade B idea rather than the other way round. It clearly indicates that entrepreneurs must provide inspiration and direction. Also, they must be able to create organizations to sustain growth. The owner of an independent small business must wear several hats at once—leading, managing and administering the new enterprise. The career prospects in start-up firms are much more as it gives employees the opportunity to learn during the course of their work.

Anand, founder and CEO, www.kreeo.com, a start-up in the space of collective intelligence and semantic technology, states that the freedom to experiment, despite the risks involved and the creative satisfaction that one derives during the implementation stage are a few factors luring the aspirants towards start-ups. As aptly put by Holt, "For the corporate venture, a company "champion" must assemble a team of like-minded people capable of breathing life into an innovation". For the high growth new venture, an entrepreneur must have the foresight to find partners or hire people with complementary skills required to guide the enterprise towards success. A business venture must be legally structured in such a way to reflect a logical organization consistent with the firm's purpose. A small tailor shop, for example, is unlikely to establish a corporation with a complex board of directors while an aerospace manufacturer would not like to have a sole proprietorship with unlimited accountability vested in one person. However, the choice of a legal form of business, its organizational structure, and the entrepreneurial team all rely on a complex set of conditions.

The performance of founding entrepreneurs determines the success or failure of new ventures. An innovative product positioned in the best possible market shall have no life of its own without a skilled founder. It is the strength of an entrepreneurial team or the ability of a committed entrepreneur that breathes life into an enterprise. Moreover, investors and bankers carefully evaluate the founder or the team that initiates to determine the chances of success for the venture. Financiers also always prefer seeing a skilled team in place rather than an individual effort though they put tremendous weight on the leadership role of the focal person who instigated the venture. Initiators are responsible for defining their businesses and identifying human resource requirements. Thus, founders must first understand their own skills and limitations. They are able to attract others to the venture. A physicist who has the knowledge to invent new technology may one day revolutionise the industry, yet if he lacks marketing acumen, his inventions will possibly never be commercially developed. Likewise, an enthusiastic entrepreneur skilled in sales who runs to market without a solid business idea may do little more than waste energy running in circles. Occasionally, an individual comes along who is capable in all these areas, but more often, entrepreneurs must face the reality of needing help. Consequently, an entrepreneurial team is needed. The lead entrepreneur must have the human resource skills to organize this team and to focus its efforts on fulfilling the venture's objectives.

CROSS-FUNCTIONALITY AND TEAM INNOVATION

Cross-functionality is the coming together of a unified cultural mindset where all functions and departments work synergistically towards enabling the growth of the enterprise. According to few empirical analysis conducted recently, there is a positive relationship between cross-functionality and team innovation. In every organization, cross-functionality has been a rising trend. Team managers put together a team of diverse people and assign them with different responsibilities.

Besides, cross-functionality, if encouraged, can also be a contributor to the personal growth of the employee as the experience enhances their professional skills outside their line of expertise. Now-a-days, in most futuristic organizations, being a cross-functional employee has become an important pre-requisite. It means that when in an organization, the employees are expected or given a chance to work in different departments so as to get a feel of how the other departments outside one's field of expertise function. Even though it is a very well accepted practice, very few organizations follow it in India. Indian organizations need to encourage this practice as a regular HR activity instead of treating it as an additional exercise.

BUILDING THE CORE TEAM AND RETENTION OF KEY EMPLOYEES

Almost every successful venture has one common thread. High or low talent or not, experienced or not, they had a group of people who stayed through the thick and thin, gave their whole to the venture and became the pillars on which the organization grew. Till any venture reaches a certain scale when momentum takes over and people start flooding to work for the company, it is irretrievable for this core group of people who are key to the company's growth. They provide stability, they act as ambassadors and lend their shoulders for the company to grow upon. Building this core team has become the biggest challenge in the context of today's job market which is very hot and where good talent will find ample offers and that too lucrative. The real challenge there in lives with an entrepreneur to provide the glue to make them stick, offer them rewards as they grow with the venture and to give them intangible reasons to stay put. It could even be personal bonding with the key employees. A really key challenge as this tests the people skills to the utmost.

EMPLOYEESHIP AND INDIAN CORPORATE CLIMATE

The success of a business venture is not only solely reliant on great leadership, but also by a level of unparalled investments made by the employee in terms of responsibility, loyalty, commitment and initiative. Employee loyalty, commitment, and responsibility are the key factors. "In terms of loyalty, loyal employees become brand exactly what is expected without being asked or made explicit". However, more often than not, questions constantly asked include, "How do we mobilize the energies of employees to create consistent success?". In the heart of this question lies the need to create an eco-system that enables employees to bring their 'hearts to work'—to get fully committed and create an organization that is built to last. This is what may be understood as employeeship.

Moreover, organizations today seek to develop a culture of ownership and responsibility. With the blink of an eye, and click of a button, we have stepped into a whole new business where change is inevitable, technology is the monster that rules all, and above all, employees have become the fulcrum of the business turf. Corporate India has undergone a facelift and so, gone are the days where the employers were the most/sole fundamental realm of the business province. When business gurus were harping on what an employer should do to keep his/her employee engaged, employeeship raised questions such as, "What should an employee do to get himself/herself?". Also, regarded as corporate citizenship for the employee, employeeship have forced corporates to wake up and smell the coffee. Thus, employeeship, in simple terms, is about creating an atmosphere that urges individuals to develop through their work and synergise with others to accomplish greater goals jointly than individually, thereby making the achievement of organizational goals greater than the mere attainment of individual goals.

HOW CAN TEAMS ACHIEVE SYNERGY?

Simply defined, synergy means the whole is greater than the sum of its parts. It means the relationship which the parts have to each other is a part in and of itself. It is not only a part, but also the most catalytic, the most empowering, the most unifying and the most exciting part. After World War II, the United Stastes commissioned David Lilienthal to head the new Atomic Energy Commission. Lilienthal brought together a group of people who were highly influential; celebreties in their own rights. This diverse group of individuals had an extremely heavy agenda and they were impatient to get at it. But Lilienthal took several weeks to create a high emotional bank account so as to speak. He had these people get to know each other, their interests, their hopes, goals, concerns, backgrounds, frames of reference and paradigms. He facilitated the kind of human interaction that creates great bonding between people and he was also heavily criticized for taking his time to do it and because it was not seemingly 'efficient'. However, the net result was that this group became closely knit together, open with each other, creative and synergistic.

Moreover, when two pieces of wood join together, they will hold much more than the total weight held by each separately. One plus one equals three or more. The challenge of course is to apply the principles of creative cooperation, which we learn from nature, in our social interactions and more specifically in our corporate work, which involves teams and the management of synergy. According to Kaicker, the Executve CMD of FranklinCovey, SouthAsia and RCS, South Asia, "My experience working with some of the leading corporations in the country shows that often teams in large format organizations (or even in mid- and small-sized firms) are focused on very narrowly defined agendas that may not include a synergistic perspective. For example, the accounting team will insist on ways, that make no sense to marketing or marketing will make absurd promises to customers, that production cannot deliver on. Teams often land up winning small battles, but lose the larger war at hand. This results in negative synergy being created in the organisastion.

The missing link in all these teams is a common larger purpose. And usually, the common larger perspective is 'What is the organisation's output and how can teams support that? What is the common goal all parties can pursue? What are the benefits of achieving that common larger purpose?. These benefits, which are clearly defined and communicated make team members see the value of a synergistic approach. Synergy in teams involves discipline and bonding and takes time. Synergistic teams are teams that perform, that deliver and that create value for their companies.

Happy companies are more efficient and make more money. Imagine for a moment how it would feel to lie on bed on a Monday morning going, "Yes ! I get to go to work this week !". Imagine what it would mean for your company, if this is how most employees felt most days. Is it possible to be this happy at work? Can we go to work and be energized, have fun, do great work, enjoy the people we work with, woo our customers, be proud of what we do, and look forward to our Monday mornings as much as some people long for Friday afternoons? Can we create workplaces where this level of happiness is the norm, not the exception?

Anyone can be happy at work, and they should be, because happy companies have:

Higher Productivity   Happy people achieve better results

Higher Quality   Happy employees care about quality

Lower Absenteeism   People actually go to work

Less Stress and Burnout   Happy people are less prone to stress

The Best People   People want to work for happy firms

Higher Sales   Happy people are best sales people

Higher Customer satisfaction   Happy employees are the best basis for good service

More adaptability   Happy people are much more adaptive and open to change

More creativity and innovation   Happy people are more creative and innovative

Better stock performances and higher profits For all of the above reasons

Undoubtedly, happy organizations/institutions make people happy, which is, of course, a goal in itself. Happiness at work is not rocket science. It does not come on its own. Every organization, leader, a manager and employee should be involved in creating a happy place through a happy team of people at work.

CONCLUSION

A group and team could only work to achieve organization's goals and objectives, if managers possess and demonstrate leadership qualities that may make team members perceive themselves as partners in progress with general acceptable interests. These will make them to share common goals that could generate ideas and energies in them that could be used for the achievement of organizational goals and objectives. In Research and Development and technological driven organizations, Burns and Stalker (1961) and Cohen and Jaffe (1982) points out that improved organization performance is contingent on human resource innovation and productivity. An organization where its human resource is neither productive nor innovative cannot survive in the changing and dynamic environment. It will position itself far away from reality and be destroyed by the whirl wind of change (Foster, 1985, 1986).

A HAPPY TEAM IS A PRODUCTIVE TEAM

When one thinks of performance, we often think of matrix, which deals with timelines, deliverables or quantitative variables that a company or a person delivers. Often, we focus a large part of our energies on such results, reviewing them, modifying them and tracking them. In fact, this is definitely a viable and required practice; but within context of a team, there are few factors that influence and enhance team performance while these factors have a different approach. Unfortunately, these parameters are, more often than not, ignored by corporate managers, who are then left wondering why teams do under-perform. The first and most important factor that impacts teams is trust. A team that lacks trust is found repeatedly delivering sub-standard results. Research shows that high performing teams achieve superior levels of participation, cooperation and collaboration for their members trust each other sharing a strong sense of identity. A team leader, thus, needs to ensure that this factor is infused into the team and wider organization. A higher level of trust, indeed, raises the pressure to perform. No one wants to let down a trusting boss and its human nature to want to deliver results when you are given the tools and are expected to perform. Similarly, employees trust the boss to ensure their career is on the right path. However, a clarification, trust can be defined as a combination of a person's character and competence.

The second factor that enhances team performance is engagement. For example, in a pharmaceutical company, the department of R & D was so excited about their work that they made one innovation and new product often with no correlation to the company's stated goal, while it was to find cheaper alternatives and processes for their current product line. This articulated corporate goal would have led to a greater market share and thus, higher profits. However, the R&D department was engaged in a separate disparate activity. The second dimension is that the team leader or the boss needs to be someone who involves him or her in team development. The leader needs to ensure that he/she is giving continuous feedback to all members, thus contributing to their ongoing development and helping them acquire new skills and competencies. An employee does not come to work everyday not only to gain monetary benefits, but also to make a difference and contribution.

SUGGESTED READINGS

1. Adair, J. (1989). Effective Team Building, Aldershot, Gower..

2. Amit, R. and Belcourt, M. (1999), Human Resource Management and Value Creating Source of Competitive Advantage, European Management Journal, vol.17(2).

3. Bass, B.M. (1960). Leadership Psychology and Organizational Behaviour, New York: Harper and Row.

4. Burns, B. and Stalker, G.M. (1961). The management Innovation, London, and Tavistock

5. Cohen, A.R. (1990). Managing People: The R-Factor, In The portable MBA, Collins, E.G.C. and Devanna, M.A.(ed.), Safari Book Exports Ltd. With Spectrum Books Ltd. (Nigeria), John Wiley and Sons.

6. Cohen, S.L. and Jaffe, C.L. (1982). Managing Human Performance for Productivity, Training and Development Journal.

7. Dauda, Y.A. (2000). Investments in Technological Innovation and Improved Productivity of The Nigerian Telecommunication. Ph.D. Thesis, University of Ibadan, Nigeria.

8. Foster, R.N. (1985)., Improving the return on R and D. Research Technology.

9. Nelson, Inc. Shavers, C.L. (1996). Technology is Always People Issue. Research Technology.

13

SOCIAL ENTREPRENEURSHIP

INTRODUCTION

Social entrepreneurship, though not a new concept, has gained renewed currency in a world characterised by a growing divide between the haves and have-nots. As discussed in the earlier chapters, entrepreneurs are, no doubt, highly motivated, innovative and critical thinkers. In addition to these qualities, when one has some drives to solve social problems, a social entrepreneur is said to be in making. Social entrepreneurs alone cannot change the world. They need artists, volunteers, development directors, communication specialists, donors, and advocates across all sectors to turn their groundbreaking ideas into reality. They need fundraisers, supporters who can change policies, someone to create a brochure describing their work. If everyone wants to start a new organization, who is going to do all the work? Whether it is to launch organizations to improve education in Africa, to better the livelihood of women in inner city Chicago, or solve any number of other big problems. It's clear that this field has captured the imagination of the Millennial generation. From Babson to Berkeley, students today can take a variety of courses on social entrepreneurship, as a minor in the subject, and will soon be able to major in it. It's time to help young people see the variety of ways and venues in which they can have a social impact. Today, B-schools offer substantive programs at the graduate level, when just a few years ago such a thing was unheard of.

Do you work for a leading company? Are you responsible for launching a new initiative, product/service, or business model that is a force for good in the world? Would your colleagues describe you as someone who pushes boundaries and has the potential to be at the forefront of social change given the opportunity and resources? If so, you may be a social intrapreneur! Social intrapreneurs are becoming instigators in the race towards a new kind of economy. These changemakers are developing innovative and scalable solutions to some of the world's most pressing problems ranging from health to education to environment. But contrary to social entrepreneurs, they are innovating from within some of the world's largest companies. Delivering game-changing innovation inside a company is never easy, but it is even more challenging when the problems you are tackling—such as climate change or poverty—are not always well-understood or overtly connected to the business strategy.

Social entrepreneurs play a crucial role in addressing social issues with their innovative solutions. They bring in wide ranging changes while tackling the pressing and daunting social issues. Be it Nobel laureate, Muhammad Yunus (Bangladesh), Bunker Roy (India) or Florence Nightingale (U.K.), they have all the way been the game-changers. In essence, social entrepreneurs have proved to be the pioneers who benefit the humanity at large. As a change agent, they have a catalytic role in order to effect social transformation. However, the characteristics of social entrepreneurs may be discussed in the following manner.

CHARACTERISTICS OF SOCIAL ENTREPRENEUR

i. **Ambitious**   With a mission, social entrepreneurs are found to be highly ambitious. Their style of functioning proves to be those of the reformers. They work in different spheres of activity while handling myriad social problems. They can do so through social purpose ventures, viz., hybrid organizations mixing attributes of non-profit and for-profit organizations, for-profit community development banks, etc.

ii. **Objective-oriented**   Social entrepreneurs strive hard to have significant transformation accompanied by tangible result. With the requisite skill to harness the society potential, they even transform the age-old equilibrium opening new vistas for socio-economic progress.

iii. **Strategic**   Social entrepreneurs search and locate to issues confronting a society. With their perseverance, they intervene with new solutions while utilizing the existing problem as an opportunity.

iv. **Missionary Attitude**   In creating value for the society they serve, hardly they look for any return, though wealth may be generated in the process of their effort. The attitude and zeal they have like that of a missionary help them stand an organisation out of their own courage and fortitude. In essence, "social entrepreneurs are not content just to give a fish or teach how to fish. They will not rest until they have revolutionized the fishing industry (www.skollfoundation. org)".

v. **Resourceful** Unlike a business entrepreneur, a social entrepreneur works within a social framework. He never takes interest in the world of business. With their limited capital, they are always on the look out for mobilizing political, financial and human resources to solve their targeted problems.

SOCIAL ENTREPRENEURSHIP AND INCLUSIVE GROWTH

Undoubtedly, social entrepreneurship has been increasingly a socio-economic phenomenon in the recent years. It has proved to have one of the unique contributions for inclusive growth at the micro level. At the same time, social entrepreneurs are those who identify the problems of the society through an intensive investigation, appropriate experiment by consistently innovating for an apt solution of an issue. Social entrprueners rightly serve the society in two different methods as mentioned below.

There are, in fact, two types of social purpose enterprises, such as, affirmative business and direct-service business. The former has a thrust on creating economic wealth as well as the jobs for those who are mentally, physically challenged, educationally and economically disadvantaged people at comparatively the lower strata of the society. Social enterprises play the role of a change agent being instrumental to bring the deprived and marginalized people to join the mainstream, whereas, the latter kind of business leads to development through community-based training and nurturing. Such community-based training include vocational training, life skills and job training as well. However, the care services are provided like child/adult care, training for the disadvantaged, garden and home maintenance.

CONSTRAINTS OF SOCIAL ENTREPRENEURSHIP

Social entrepreneurs face numerous problems. For example, bureaucratic headaches happen in every country. Social enterprises are particularly vulnerable to such obstacles, especially if the start-up disrupts the status quo and must then defend itself against resistance by entrenched interests. Seemingly, projects are marred by one or more instances of official inertia, corruption, lack of support or bureaucratic foot-dragging. For instance, you might complete all the appropriate application forms to start a business, only to be told no by the local authorities, that too with no explanation. In one case, a social entrepreneur had an idea that could significantly enhance medical services in a country hard hit by HIV/AIDS. His idea was first to computerize all medical records, eventually build an expert system, and then train nurses to do diagnostic and prescription work, which was being handled by the country's limited pool of highly overloaded doctors. To anyone looking from the outside, it seemed like a win-win-win.

Therefore, he was shaken by the negative responses to his proposed idea. Reactions from people in the health department, in local hospitals, and in public clinics ranged from complete indifference to outright hostility. He then learned that two years earlier, a well-established local subsidiary of a multi-national software and consulting firm had sold a full-service healthcare management system to the country's health department. The system had then been force-launched in a number of public hospitals and clinics, at great expense, and was simply not working as hoped. The post-installation challenges had caused major disruptions in healthcare delivery, thereby creating a highly dissatisfied set of stakeholders, who were justifiably disillusioned and disgruntled. This entrepreneur was nearly derailed in the very beginning by unexpected negative feedback from key stakeholders. Such poor political savvy has destroyed many a well-intentioned enterprise. That is why every start-up needs a socio-political strategy. Having learnt the dynamics and dimensions of social enterprenuership, we can look into few amazing and successful social entrepreneurs of India and abroad.

SOCIAL ENTREPRENEURSHIP IN PRACTICE

For better understanding, selected cases of social entreprennuer/ entrepreneurship along with the origin and their features are given below:

Dr. Achyuta Samanta, A New Gen Social Entrepreneur in Odisha

The founder of Kaling Institute of Industrial Technolgy University, Bhubaneswar, Dr. Samanta has made long strides in the field of higher education in Odisha vis-a-vis India. His dream university as a not-for-profit organization has faced a myriad of challenges since its inception two decades ago. KIIT has been synergizinng social values with scientific knowledge through as many as 40 programmes ranging from management to engineering and medicine. As a celebrated social entrepreneur, he urges the KIIT products to try their level best in order to give away a small portion of their comfort and knowledge to the deprived sections of the community. In his opinion, it would certainly be like giving sight to the visually impaired persons in the society.

Bangladesh Rural Advancement Committee (BRAC)

The BRAC was established in 1972 by Fazle Abed, a Bangladeshi corporate executive, in the aftermath of the

Independence War. Over the years, BRAC has focused on breaking the cycle of poverty in Bangladesh. Starting as a relief and resettlement organization, BRAC pioneered the development of comprehensive, locally organized approaches to rural development and poverty alleviation. It provides a range of services- rural capacity–building, education, health services, and micro-credit to 2.6 million rural people. It has had fleeting success in developing projects that contribute to its own financial sustainability.

- Essential Innovation: Focuses on local requirement and capacities through a systemic approach to poverty alleviation that emphasizes a kind of multi-level learning process. Instituted rapid scaling up of the organization while ensuring sustainability.

- Scope: Operation in 60,000 of the 86,000 villages in Bangladesh. Organizes the poor for self-help and builds local capacities for economic development alongwith education and health. Seeks to change local attitudes and culture for the land less with a thrust on working with women and other deprived people.

Self Employed Women's Association (SEWA)

Under SEWA instituted in 1972 by Ela Bhatt, hawkers and vendors, home-based producers, manual labourers and service providers were organized for improvement of their working conditions with the help of police and policy makers. It, further, provided a variety of services to its members, it being the first and largest trade union of informal sector workers.

Essential Innnovation Organizing the women workers, it builds local leadership capacity to expand and activize movement and organization.

Scope Influenced the International Labour Organization to frame standards for the home-makers. Self-employed women in large numbers became members of the union. Also, co-founded international network in order to support the labour and its dignity in the female informal sector.

The Grameen Bank (GB)

Established in 1976, the founder of GB, Prof. Yunus, stated that the poor are also bankable, even landless women groups can achieve a high rate of repayment. Instead of collateral, GB constitutes groups of five people to provide mutual and morally binding group guarantee. These members in group have their credit worthiness without being defaulters for repayment of their loan. Further, becoming small entrepreneurs have helped to be economically independent and for a better self-sufficient livelihood. Under this Grameen system, members follow the social development guidelines called 'sixteen decisions'.

Essential Innovation Provides lending for the poor with no collateral.

Scope Created a sound premise around the world for women's role in income generating activities (IGA) as well as for implementation of micro-credit practices.

CONCLUSION

Social entrepreneurs are, undoubtedly, visionaries in their approach and style. Without any profit motive, they are committed to the cause of the deprived and disadvantaged section of the society. They come with innovative ideas that results in enduring benefits to the target groups. In a nutshell, like their business counterparts, they search for novel and better ways to address issues that plague the society. As history speaks, such individuals have introduced solutions to seemingly intractable social problems, fundamentally improving the lives of the poorer class towards a better future.

SUGGESTED READINGS

1. Khanka, S.S. (1998): Entrepreneurial Development, S. Chand, New Delhi.

2. Wallace, S.Levonda (1999)

14

PROBLEMS OF ENTREPRENEURSHIP

INTRODUCTION

Entrepreneurship as a career should never be viewed as a bed of roses. If one overcomes an already existing problem, a new one starts emerging. The entrepreneur faces problems in the beginning. He is also beset with problems when the enterprise is alive and kicking. Here, we can rightly quote Martin Luther King who has said, "The ultimate measure of a man is not where he stands in moments of comfort and convinience, but where he stands at times of challenge and controversy." Keeping this in mind, the problems of an entrepreneur can be discussed as external and internal problems. Every business is affected by externalities: economic business cycles, fluctuating interest rates, inflation, trends in the labour market, interrupted supplies, government regulations and unstable financial markets.

External problems arise from factors beyond the control of the entrepreneur, whereas internal problems are hardly influenced by external forces. However, the problems of industries, whether small or otherwise are almost identical.

An organised enterprise is financially strong, its resources being comparatively larger. It has, thus, an advantage of tackling problems more effectively. While the large sector firm can employ trained and experienced managers, in the small sector, the firm's proprietor or the partners, or if the unit is a company, its director or directors have to handle all the problems. The former can influence its raw material suppliers, its customers, and at times even the Government, but the latter, more often than not, proves to be helpless. He, therefore, has to sort out the entire range of problems despite a myriad of issues confronted by him. A general rise in consumer prices will reduce sales. A similar rise in producer price will inflate costs. It is the smaller enterprise which is far more susceptible to these forces than a large firm. For instance, IBM has easy access to capital resources to tide over a recession, but a local contractor may run out of cash and go under.

Furthermore, a major toy manufacturer may be able to find alternative financing on the face of soaring rate of interest, but the local toy store may watch its profit evaporate due to sheer debt obligations. Also, opportunities in small business are distinct from those of high growth enterprises. Small businesses are those started by individuals who seek income substitution while serving a local constituency. Therefore, most small business owners are not concerned with changing the world, finding a cure for the common cold, or setting the industry on its heel with some marvellous new invention. To the contrary, they are concerned with filling immediate needs of their customers and clients within the scope of well-defined markets.

ENTREPRENEURIAL PROBLEMS

INTERNAL	EXTERNAL
(i) Entrepreneur's idea	(i) Infrastructural
(ii) Faulty Planning	(a) Location
(iii) Poor project implementation	(b) Power
(iv) Inefficient management	(c) Water
(v) Poor production	(d) Communication
(vi) Poor quality	(ii) Financial
(vii) Marketing	(a) Capital
(viii) Labour Issues	(b) Working Capital
(ix) Inadequate finance	(c) Long-term Funds
	(d) Recovery
(x) Capacity Utilization	(iii) Marketing
(xi) Inadequate Training	(iv) Raw material
(xii) Ineffective organisation	(v) Taxation
(xiii) Lack of strategies	(vi) Industrial Regulations
(xiv) Lack of vision	(vii) Inspection
(xv) Lack of motivation	(viii) Technology
(xvi) Inadequate connections	(ix) Government Policy

PROBLEMS OF SMALL ENTREPRENEURS: WHY AND HOW

Small scale units have, undoubtedly experienced phenomenal growth over the decades, though they suffer innumerable problems right from their births. Despite the tall talk made about several government schemes and programmes for the success of small enterprises, the concerned entrepreneurs come across innumerable obstacles since the very day of conceiving the idea to setting up an enterprise. The initial step in setting up of an enterprise, i.e., preparation of a project report needs lot of data, sometimes of a specialized nature. While a large business unit can afford to pay decently to a consultant, the same thing makes it difficult for a small entrepreneur. Further, in India, various institutions promote and assist small entrepreneurs, whereas, lack of proper coordination among them have caused small business units sick due to the following reasons:

i.   Delayed infrastructural provisions, such as, sheds, power, road, water, etc.

ii.   Poor co-ordination between the State Financial Corporations and lending banks.

iii. Lack of expertise of the bank officials.

iv.   Compliance of a large number of legal provisions as regards taxation, labour and excise.

v.   Inadequacy of required technical support to the entrepreneur.

vi.   Bank funds being bad debt for selecting inefficient entrepreneur.

vii. Delays in bill payment leading to liquidity problem.

viii. Overlapping of the items reserved for purchase from the small enterprises.

ix.   Higher risk of small enterprises becoming sick on natural grounds.

Given some specific reasons behind the sickness of small units, it would be pertinent to examine below some definitions of sickness:

As put by Sick Industrial Companies Act, 1985, an industrial company is defined as sick if:

i.   it was registered for at least 7 years;

ii.   it incurred cash loss for the current and the preceding year; and

iii.   its net worth was eroded. According to the Industrial Development Bank of India, "A unit may be considered sick, if it has defaulted the payment of three instalments. Besides, the Reserve Bank of India has defined in the following words: "A sick unit is one which has incurred a cash loss for the year and is likely to continue cash loss for the current year as well as in the following year and the unit has an imbalance in its financial structure, such as current ratio is less than one and there is a widening trend in the debt-equity ratio, i.e., total outside liabilities to net worth."

However, the Reserve Bank of India has viewed sickness with much concern, it set up Kohli Committee which has defined in the following words: "A small scale industrial unit is considered as sick when,

i.   If any of the borrowal accounts of the unit remains substandard for more than six months, i.e., principal or interest in respect of any of the borrowal accounts has remained overdue for a period exceeding one year will remain unchanged even if the present period for classification of an account as substandard is reduced in due course, or

ii.   There is erosion in the net worth due to accumulated losses to the extent of 50 per cent of its net worth during the previous accounting year, and

iii.   The unit has been in commercial production for at least two years."

In India, a rewarding feature of economic development has been the impressive growth entrepreneurs, particularly, in the MSE sector. At the same time, rapid industrial growth has brought in its wake incidence of sickness in this sector. Needless to say, sickness is a gradual process which does not have an instant occurrence. However, sickness can be of three types as given below:

i. **Genuine sickness** It is beyond the control of the entrepreneur as such a phenomenon is unavoidable.

ii. **Incipient sickness** It is a case when the capacity utilization is below 50 per cent of the highest achieved during the preceding five years.

iii. **Induced sickness** It happens to be the reason behind high incidence of sickness. The relevant causes in this case are more internal than external. This may be termed as man-made as unscrupulous managers/promoters may deliberately cause this to occur.

CAUSES OF INDUSTRIAL SICKNESS

As mentioned earlier, some of the factors behind sickness are beyond the control of the unit. Yet, there are factors originating from within the unit. These two categories are known as exogenous factors and endogenous factors. Accordingly, we can make a discussion of the factors of both the categories with significant impacts on the enterprises.

Financial Constraints

The very availabity of adequate finance makes it possible to hire labour, arrange material, buy machine and equipments for a business unit. Due to various reasons, such as, rigidity or policy of credit restriction by the financial institutions or promoters's failure to comply with some unrealistic conditions imposed by the financial institutions, business units do not avail their fund requirements. This type of situation will result in industrial sickness for the reasons like failure to maintain the desired level of liquidity by the firm.

Marketing Constraints

Marketing is the sine qua non for the success of any enterprise. Hardly, it makes any sense to go for any sort of production, if there is no effective marketing strategy or adequate number of takers for a product. In the natural process, a firm suffers from sickness due to want of demand for its product thereby leading to a fall in the revenue earning. Particularly, for a small firm, the revenue may go down due to shrinking in demand, if it fails to compete effectively with its competitors in the mediunm and large-scale sector. It may, also suffer from the expectation of its markets in terms of product quality, price, design and other specifications. An economic slowdown leading to sluggish market demand may have significant impact on the demand of a concern's product. However, in case of bulk purchases made from this concern by specific organizations, viz., Defense or Departments of Government, some policy changes may create bottleneck in the demand for the firm's product.

Production Constraints

A firm's production process faces a likely setback in case of non-availability of the inputs of desired quantity and quality due to government restrictions or other environmental forces. Shortage of power, water and other infrastructural inputs put undue pressure on the production process When the firm is unable to maintain its production or a product substitute, the unit is bound to witness its sickness.

Manpower Constraints

The firm's manpower is the most crucial factor of production as the use of material, machine and finance depends upon the quality of the human capital. Non-availabilty of quality manpower is bound to affect the fate of an enterprise including a small firm. Absence of skilled man-power and conditions of general labour supply is likely to impede the growth causing firm's sickness. Persistent labour problems including industrial unrest come on the way of a firm's success. It also amounts to rising overhead costs, unwanted wastage, poorer quality production. Such production as well as lesser productivity may be caused directly due to ineffective use of the manpower.

GOVERNMENT POLICIES

Any policy changes made by the government within a short span of time, as in case of licensing, import, limit of credit or taxation may turn a viable firm sick. For instance, if the line of demarcation between products to be produced by the small firms and the large firms is removed, it will lead to unhealthy competition between the two. Similarly, government policy to raise the import restriction may allow foreign qualitative goods at cheaper rate causing sickness for the small firms.

Lack of Infrastructure

A firm's cost of production is adversely affected thereby reducing its bargaining power due to absence of adequate infrastructural facilities. This leads to low profitability strongly exihibiting a case of industrial sickness.

Inability to avail Credit Loans

A small firm for its lower scale of production enjoys a poor bargaining power with its supplier. Being unable to make bulk purchases, it has to suffer from adverse terms of credit without the advantage of discount and concession. At the same time, its customers demand to make purchases on longer terms of credit alongwith rebate, discount and concession.

Working Capital Constraints

More often than not, executives in the financial institutions handling the issues like finance supplied to small firms fail to make a complete evaluation of a project. Sometimes, it takes almost a year to avail a short term loan from a commercial bank. Due to heavy investments made already by an entrepreneur, it is, indeed difficult to neglect the project due to want of shot term credit. As a result, the enterprise faces working capital constraints leading to irrecoverable delays in commercial production.

Internal Causes

Instances are galore to note that small units are chiefly beset with external factors while medium and large scale units are plagued by internal factors like poor management or mismanagement. However, majority of projects suffer due to innumerable internal causes, like poor management, shortage of working capital, labour and other problems. Problems of poor management, paucity of working capital, poor implementation, operational and labour problems are considered to be major causes behind the failure of majority of the projects. In fact, these internal or endogenous causes are those found within the control of a unit.

Locational Disadvantage

Any disadvantage from the point of view of raw material or marketing will create unwanted difficulties for an enterprise, whether small or big. Location-wise, an enterprise needs to be suitably located. The favourable location can bring in cost advantage in terms of availability of raw material. This also helps to have easy access to the existing and potential markets alike.

Lack of Initiative and Entrepreneurial Talent

Entrepreneurship is related to personality, while, entrepreneurs necessarily belong to a special class. The initiative and talent lacking with an entrepreneur can bring the misfortune to her/his enterprise. This being the very basis behind the success of an entrepreneur speaks a lot about the firm's future. Entrepreneur's individual initiative, perseverance and commitment in organizing the firm can bring opportunity or otherwise.

Marketing Ability

Entrepreneurial ability for marketing the firm's product is of paramount importance for efficiently and profitably operating a firm. Whatever be the quality of product, only marketing ability can help to find a good number of takers for the product. In fact, the marketing strategy of a business organization can bring its desired result for a prospective future.

Product Quality

A firm's product can carry the message of the organization to the outside world; be it a manufacturing or service providing concern. The quality of the product can determine the volume of business alongwith the marketing potential. Hence, product quality needs to be maintained at any cost in this age of cut-throat competition and globalisation.

Organization and Management

Organizational ability and managerial efficiency in case of an enterprise proves to be a determining factor for an organizational success. Organizing being one of the crucial role of entrepreneur, if not done properly will have a telling effect on the functioning and future of an organization. Organisational climate must be conducive for a sound corporate culture and practice. Further, effective management of various dynamics of entrepreneurship needs to be handled properly for a sustainable and progressive enterprise.

Inter-personal Relationships

Be it group behaviour or team spirit, the environment to nurture good human relationship within and outside the organization can ever build a sound organization. Indeed, it is this kind of relationships promoted in the firm not only makes a healthy relationship among the in-house people, but also helps develop a lasting relationship between the firm and outside stake-holders including the customers. The firm may be as big as that of IBM, POSCO, Reliance Communication or General Motors or even TATA Sons, but the human relationships maintained always speaks big for the firm's success or failure.

CONCLUSION

The entrepreneurial problems have been discussed several times in this book prior to the discussion made here. However, to conclude here, we can say this much that an enterprise has to confront with problems of different nature as already mentioned in this chapter. As an old adage speaks, "where there is will, there is way". Thus, an apt and able entrepreneur needs to manage the enterprise so as to avoid problems including possible sickness.

INDEX